Knitted Socks
from Finland

First published in Great Britain 2022 by
Search Press Limited
Wellwood
North Farm Road
Tunbridge Wells
Kent TN2 3DR

Originally published as *Villasukkien uusi vuosi* in Finland
by Otava Publishing, Helsinki, Finland.

© Niina Laitinen ja Kustannusosakeyhtiö Otava 2020

English translation by Burravoe Translation Services

For the Finnish edition:
Instructions and charts: Niina Laitinen
Photographs and styling, graphic design and layout:
Viola Virtamo

ISBN: 978-1-78221-983-5
ebook ISBN: 978-1-80093-059-9

The Publishers and author can accept no responsibility for
any consequences arising from the information, advice or
instructions given in this publication.

Readers are permitted to reproduce any of the items in this
book for their personal use, or for the purposes of selling
for charity, free of charge and without the prior permission
of the Publishers. Any use of the items for commercial
purposes is not permitted without the prior permission of
the Publishers.

If you have difficulty in obtaining any of the materials and
equipment mentioned in this book, then please visit the
Search Press website for details of suppliers:
www.searchpress.com

Knitted Socks from Finland

20 Nordic designs for all year round

NIINA LAITINEN

SEARCH PRESS

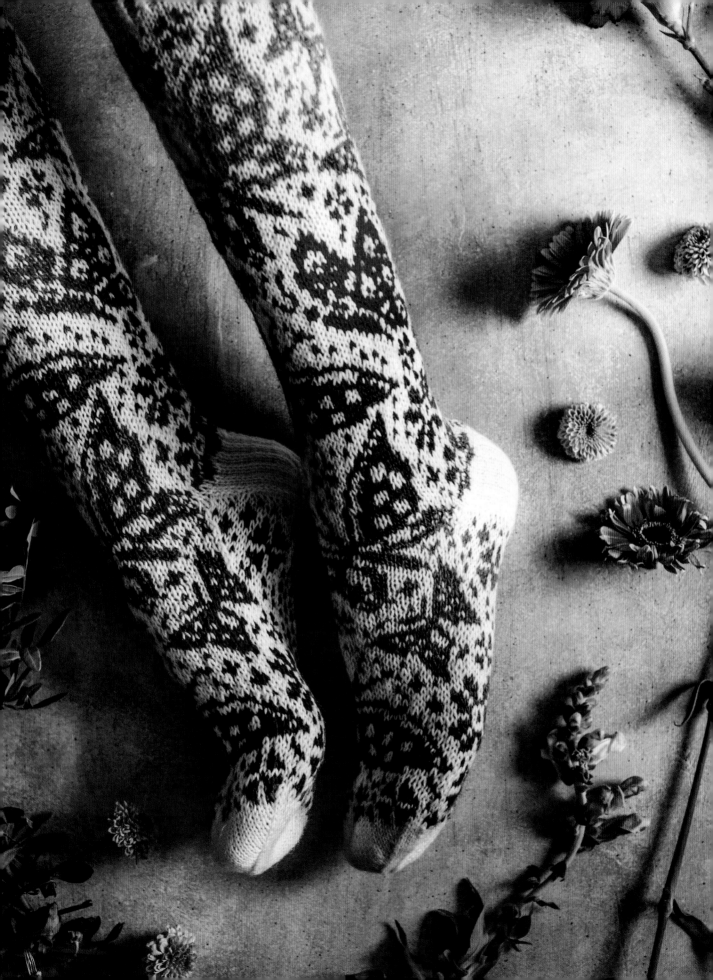

This book is dedicated to
my sisters Mari, Paula,
Reeta and Heta.

The sock designs

Fleeting Moment

SPRING

Cherry Blossom Time

SPRING

Enchanting

SPRING

May

SPRING

Happy Wanderer

SPRING

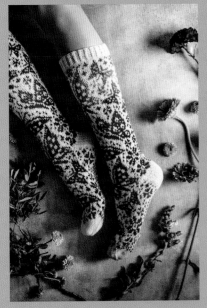

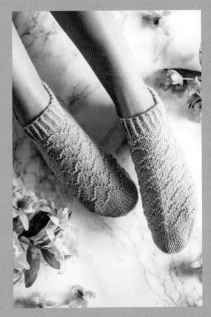

Dear Sister

SUMMER

Careless Love

SUMMER

Hair of Gold

SUMMER

Paradise

SUMMER

Wedding Waltz

SUMMER

Endless

AUTUMN

Flirtation

AUTUMN

Adventure

AUTUMN

Soulmates

AUTUMN

Lake Tiilikka

AUTUMN

Frozen Seas

WINTER

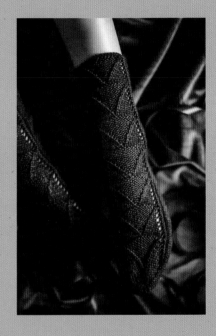

Longing

WINTER

Christmas Eve

WINTER

Secret Snowfall

WINTER

Snow Queen

WINTER

Contents

12   Foreword

14   Abbreviations and knitting tips

16   Yarn used in the book and alternatives

SPRING

20   Fleeting Moment

28   Cherry Blossom Time

40   Enchanting

48   May

54   Happy Wanderer

SUMMER

62   Dear Sister

70   Careless Love

76   Hair of Gold

80   Paradise

86   Wedding Waltz

AUTUMN

94   Endless

102   Flirtation

110   Adventure

120   Soulmates

130   Lake Tiilikka

WINTER

140   Frozen Seas

146   Longing

154   Christmas Eve

160   Secret Snowfall

166   Snow Queen

Foreword

This book is full of memories, landscapes and moments of joy. I have taken my inspiration from nature, its beauty and its secrets, and the feeling of being out in the fresh air in fair winds and foul.

The book is divided into seasons, with five sock patterns for each one and I hope you will join me on this journey through the Finnish calendar. On the cusp of spring, we appreciate the first hints of green after the snow, the return of the sun after the darkness of winter, and the magic of the cherry blossom.

In the summer, we join my sisters to revel in the light of summer nights in the north, spellbound by the natural world, as we dance to a wedding waltz. In the autumn, we head northwards with a tent, indulge in a flirtation and embark on an adventure in the wilds as the leaves quietly fall to the ground.

The magic of winter encompasses a snow queen, a peaceful Christmas and perhaps a thrill of excitement at the thought of the year to come.

I have aimed to write instructions that are easy to follow and quick to knit. A few of the patterns are slightly more challenging but I would definitely encourage you to give them a try and work them out. If you get stuck, you can always ask for advice on the Niina Laitinen designs Facebook page or in the Taimitarha Facebook group.

Once again, my heartfelt thanks to everyone who helped me while I was writing this book. Thank you for being there.

NIINA

Abbreviations

Some of the abbreviations listed here are used in every pattern and others are only used in a few designs. A key to the symbols used in the chart is shown next to each chart.

GARTER STITCH KNITTED FLAT	knit on the right and the wrong side
K	knit
K2TOG	knit 2 stitches together
LH	left hand
P	purl
P2TOG	purl 2 stitches together
RH	right hand
RS	right side of work
S1	slip 1 stitch knitwise, unless the instructions specifically state slip 1 purlwise. When using a slipped stitch pattern to reinforce the heel, you can just move the slip stitch over instead of slipping it knitwise to make the chains of stitches look neater.
SKPO	slip 1, knit 1, pass slipped stitch over to decrease. Slip 1 stitch knitwise, knit 1 stitch and pass the slipped stitch over the knitted stitch. The skpo decrease can be replaced with the ssk decrease.
S1 PURLWISE	slip 1 stitch as if you were going to purl it. Slip the stitch to the right-hand needle, keeping the yarn at the front of the work.
SL ST	slip stitch
SSK	slip, slip, knit to decrease. Slip 2 stitches one at a time knitwise onto the right-hand needle, slide the stitches back onto the left-hand needle and knit them together through the back loops. The ssk decrease can replace the skpo decrease.
ST/STS	stitch(es)
ST ST	stocking (US stockinette) stitch; knit on the right side and purl on the wrong side
STOCKING (STOCKINETTE) STITCH IN THE ROUND	knit every stitch
WS	wrong side of work
YARN OVER FROM FRONT	loop yarn over the needle from the front. Some of the patterns use this yarn over so that the new knit stitch created will be facing the right way on the next round.
YO	yarn over (loop yarn over the needle from the back)
–	repeat the part of the instructions between the asterisks

Knitting tips

HEEL ROWS	The total number of rows for the heel is always counted from the start of the reinforced heel unless the instructions state otherwise.
INCREASE	In some of the patterns one or more stitches are added for the heel flap; here, the easiest way to increase the number of stitches is to pick up the yarn between two stitches on the previous row and work into it knitwise/purlwise.
NEEDLE DIVISION	All the patterns divide the stitches between 4 double-pointed needles and almost all the patterns also state how many stitches there should be on each needle and show this on the charts. If the number of stitches per needle is not shown, then it is not important. Sometimes stitches are moved from one needle to another when increasing or decreasing and here you need to check the total number of stitches remains correct. If you prefer to use stitch markers, the needle boundary lines on the chart could be used to indicate where to place them.
NEEDLE NUMBERING	Needles 1 and 4 form the back of the sock and needles 2 and 3 form the front of the sock unless otherwise stated.
CHART READING	Charts are read from right to left and from bottom to top, unless otherwise stated.
READING LACE CHARTS	Due to the increases and decreases, in some of the lace charts the row you are knitting cannot directly be compared with the row below. To make sure the lace pattern comes out correctly, always work each row on its own without reference to the stitches in previous rows.
FAIR ISLE (STRANDED/COLOURWORK)	When knitting with two different yarns, catch in the floats (the long strands at the back of the work) every few stitches. When switching needles, it is a good idea to slightly stretch the stitches and make sure that you are not knitting too tightly.
TENSION (GAUGE)	The tension is stated at the start of each pattern. If you don't know your own tension for the particular yarn, I recommend knitting a tension swatch to measure and check. If your tension is tighter than the tension stated for the pattern, the result will be smaller socks, and vice versa.
CHANGING SIZE	The easiest way to change the size of the socks is by changing the size of your needles. Bigger needles will produce bigger socks and smaller needles will produce smaller socks. Each pattern contains instructions for different sizes or tips for changing the sizing.

Yarn used and alternatives

400–420m = 100g
recommended needle size
2.5mm (UK 12/13, US 1/2)

Used:
Drops Fabel
Kirjo-Pirkka
Lana Grossa
Louhittaren Luola Väinämöinen
Malabrigo Sock
Opal 4-ply
Regia 4-ply

Alternatives:
Alize
Austermann Step
Kaupunkilanka Keskustori
Maladi
Novita Venla
Socki Fine

250–270m = 100g
recommended needle size
3mm (UK 11, US 2/3)

Used:
Gjestal Maija
Kaupunkilanka Rotvalli
Novita Nalle
Teetee Pallas

Alternatives:
Austermann Step 6
Louhittaren Luola
  Väinämöinen sport
Nordia Oona
Opal 6-ply
Regia 6-ply
Vuorelma Veto

200m = 100g
recommended needle size
3.5mm (UK 9/10, US 4)

Used:
Gjestal Janne
Kaupunkilanka Kivijalka
Novita 7 Veljestä

Alternatives:
Adlibris Socki
Nordia Oiva
Teetee Salla

spring

Fleeting Moment

The first rays of sunlight tentatively emerging after the dark Finnish winter melt everyone's hearts. When you smile and the sun smiles back, you can sense all the joy and happiness that spring brings with it. In these socks, your face lights up as sunshine returns and you stop for a fleeting moment and watch the natural world springing back into life.

SIZE: UK 6 (Europe 39, US 8½)

YARN: 1 ball of Novita Nalle DK (8-ply/light worsted) yarn in Saffron 285; 100g/260m/284yd

AMOUNT USED: 85g (3oz)

KNITTING NEEDLES: 3mm (UK 11, US 2/3) DPN or size to obtain correct tension

TENSION (GAUGE): 23 sts and 28 rows/ 10cm (4in)

BEFORE YOU START

The right and left socks are mirror images of each other. Use charts A right and B right for the right sock and charts A left and B left for the left sock. Otherwise the instructions are the same for both socks.

In the charts for the leg, needles 1 and 2 form the front of the sock and needles 3 and 4 form the back of the sock and the heel. After the heel, the needle numbering changes and needles 1 and 4 are used for the sole of the sock and needles 2 and 3 for the top.

LEG

Cast on 60 sts and divide across 4 needles as follows: 25 sts in total on needles 1 and 2, 35 sts in total on needles 3 and 4.

Knit the leg following chart A (50 rounds). On the last round of the chart, change the number of sts on each needle by moving the first 2 sts on needle 3 to needle 2 and the last 2 sts on needle 4 to needle 1. This gives you 31 sts for the heel flap (sts on needles 3 and 4). Move the heel sts onto one needle.

HEEL

Turn the work, s1 purlwise, p1, p2tog, purl to end of row (30 sts for heel flap). Turn work.

Row 1 (RS): *s1, k1*, repeat from * to * to end of row. Turn work.
Row 2 (WS): s1 purlwise and purl to end of row. Repeat these two rows until the heel flap has 28 rows and you have completed the last WS row.

Start to decrease to turn the heel: continue in the same sl st pattern to reinforce the heel. Starting with a RS row, knit until 11 sts remain on LH needle. Decrease 1 st using ssk or skpo and turn the work, leaving 9 sts on the other needle. S1 purlwise, purl until 11 sts remain on LH needle. P2tog and turn work. S1 and continue in the sl st pattern until 10 sts remain on LH needle. Decrease using ssk or skpo and turn the work. S1 purlwise, purl until 10 sts remain on LH needle. P2tog and turn work. Continue in the same way, reducing the number of sts at the sides on each row while keeping the same number of sts in the middle (10).

When you run out of side sts, divide the heel flap sts between 2 needles (5–5). Knit 5 sts to bring the yarn to the centre of the heel, between needle 1 and needle 4.

FOOT

Pick up 16 sts from LH edge of heel flap using a spare needle. Knit the 5 sts from needle 1 and then the 16 picked up sts. Knit the sts on needles 2 and 3 following chart B starting with round 1. Pick up and knit 16 sts from RH edge of heel flap. Using the same needle, knit the 5 sts on needle 4 (71 sts).

Start the gusset decrease: at the end of needle 1, k2tog and at the start of needle 4, ssk or skpo. Decrease 2 sts in this way on every second round. Continue following chart B on needles 2 and 3. Continue decreasing the gusset sts on every second round until there are 57 sts (14–15–14–14). Continue in st st on needles 1 and 4 and in chart pattern on needles 2 and 3. Follow the chart until round 49 and then start to decrease for the toe.

The toe decrease, a wide ribbon decrease, is worked on needles 1 and 4. The chart pattern continues on needles 2 and 3.
Needle 1: knit until last 3 sts, k2tog, k1.
Needle 4: k1, ssk, k to end.
Work this decrease on every second round until there are 8 sts left on each needle. Then decrease on every round.
Needles 2 and 3: decrease for the toe following chart B (rows 50–66).

When there are 9 sts left, break off yarn and thread through the remaining sts.

Weave in ends and press lightly.

	knit		ssk: slip 2 sts one at a time knitwise, slide the sts back onto the LH needle and knit them together through back loops
Ꝙ	knit through back loop		knit 2 together
●	purl	◎	yarn over from front
o	yarn over		

CHART A: RIGHT LEG

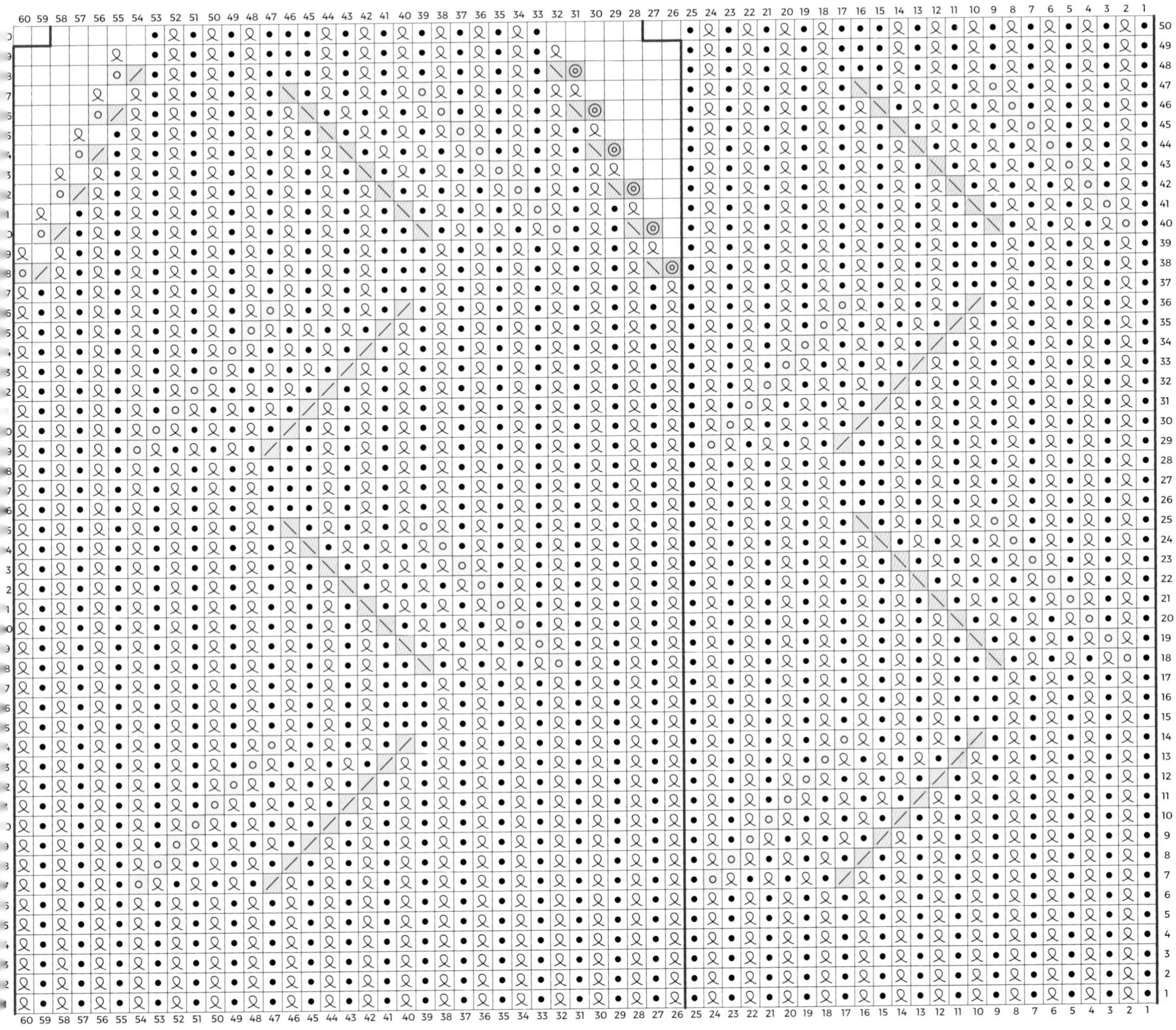

CHART B: LEFT FOOT

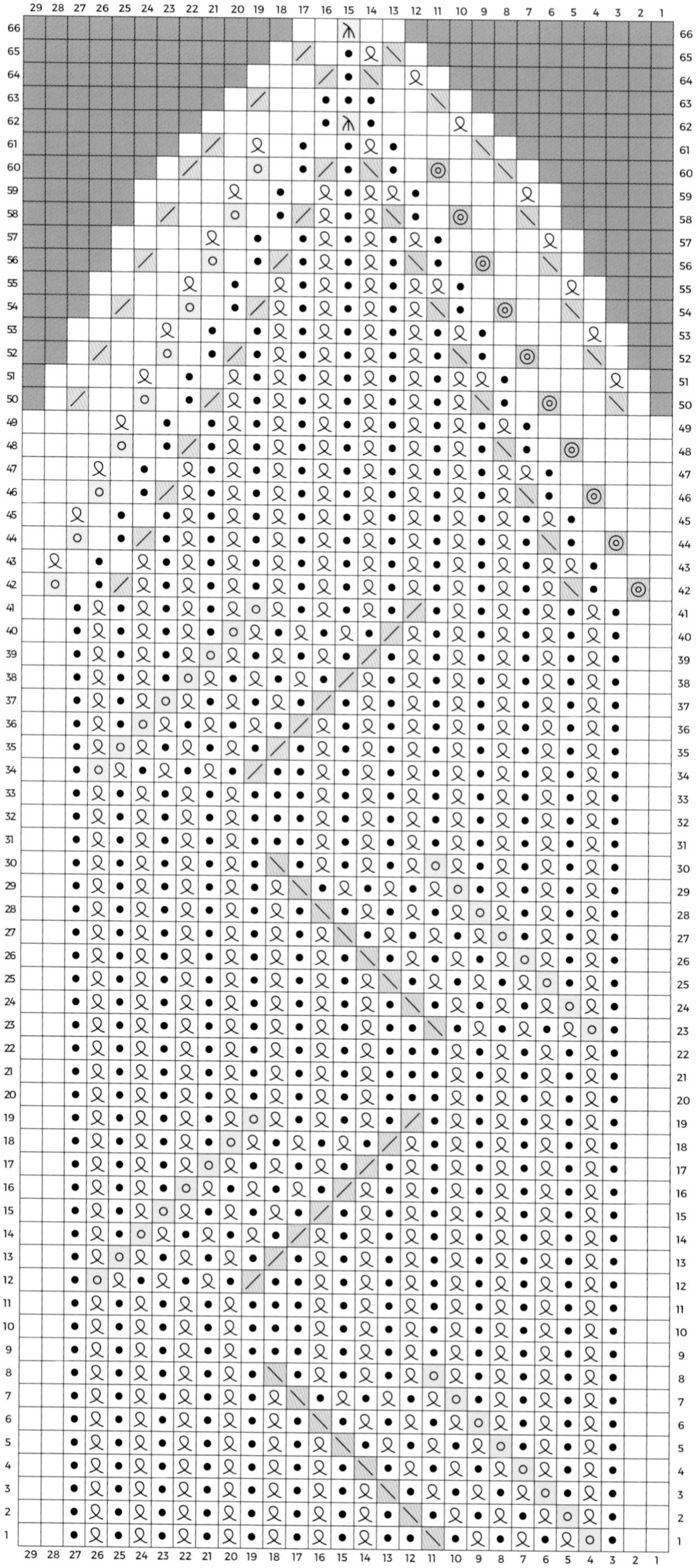

knit

knit through back loop

purl

yarn over

ssk: slip 2 sts one at a time knitwise onto RH needle, slide the sts back onto LH needle and knit them together through back loops

knit 2 together

yarn over from front

slip 1 st knitwise, knit 2 together and pass the slipped st over the knitted sts

no st

CHART B: RIGHT FOOT

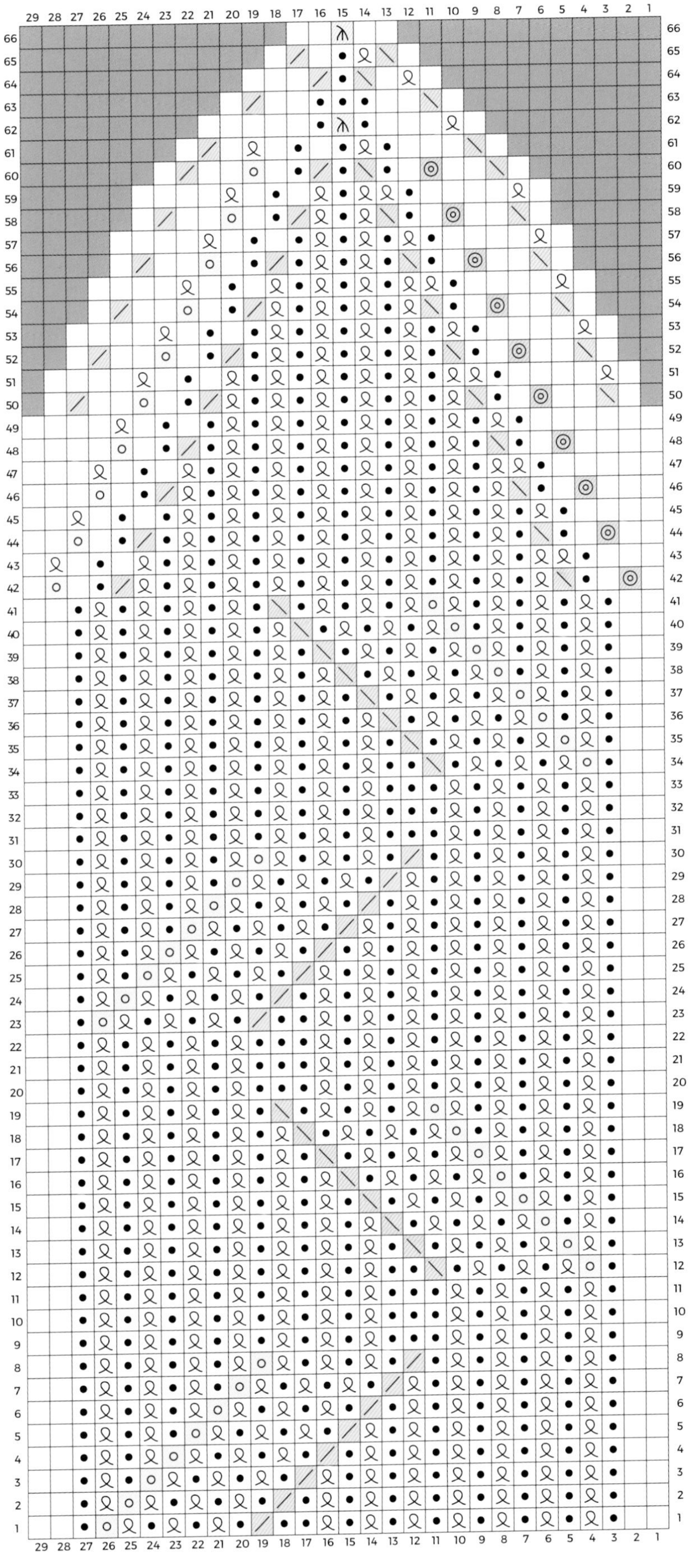

Cherry Blossom Time

Cherry blossom time, red-cheeked beneath the pink trees with a heart bursting with love. I wanted to knit wisdom, a challenge and the joy of success into these socks. The beautiful geisha's kimono meanders down to your toes, the background filled with cherry blossom and dancing petals.

SIZE: UK 6 (Europe 39, US 8½)

YARN: 1 ball each of Opal 4-ply (fingering) yarn in Black 2619 (A) and White 2620 (B); 100g/425m/465yd

AMOUNT USED: 100g (3½oz) A, 50g (1¾oz) B

KNITTING NEEDLES: 2.5mm (UK 12/13, US 1/2) DPN or size to obtain correct tension

TENSION (GAUGE): 31 sts and 33 rows/ 10cm (4in)

BEFORE YOU START
The chart is read from bottom to top and from right to left. The right and left socks are mirror images of each other. Use charts A1, B1 and C1 for the right sock and charts A2, B2 and C2 for the left sock.

LEG

Cast on 84 sts in yarn A and divide sts so you have 21 on each needle. Join, being careful not to twist, and work in the round. Start in rib following chart A and knit 14 rounds in rib.

After the rib, start the Fair Isle pattern at chart round 15. Increase 5 sts on round 15 and then divide sts across 4 needles as follows: 22–23–22–22 (89 sts). Work leg following chart, decreasing in a suitable place at beginning of needle 1 and end of needle 4 on the following rounds:

Decrease on rounds: 38, 46, 53, 58, 66, 73, 79, 89, 97, 101, 104 and 107 (65 sts).
Note: on round 80 change the number of sts on each needle to 21–17–16–21.

When you have worked all 120 rounds for the leg, divide sts between needles as follows: 16–17–16–16.

HEEL

Start heel flap in yarn A by knitting the sts on needle 1 onto needle 4 (32 heel flap sts). Leave remaining sts on needles 2 and 3. Turn work, s1 purlwise and purl to end of row. Turn work.

Row 1 (RS): *s1, k1*, repeat from * to * to end of row. Turn work.
Row 2 (WS): s1 purlwise and purl to end of row. Repeat these two rows until heel flap has 32 rows and you have completed the last WS row.

Start to decrease to turn heel: continue in the same sl st pattern to reinforce heel. Starting with a RS row, knit until there are 11 sts left on LH needle. Decrease 1 st using ssk or skpo and turn work leaving 9 sts on the other needle. S1 purlwise and purl until 11 sts remain on LH needle. P2tog and turn work. S1 and continue in sl st pattern until there are 10 sts left on LH needle. Decrease using ssk or skpo and turn work. S1 purlwise and purl until 10 sts remain on

LH needle. P2tog and turn work. Continue in the same way, reducing the number of sts at the sides on each row and keeping the same number of sts (12) in the middle.

When you run out of side sts, divide the heel flap sts between 2 needles (6–6). K6 to bring yarn to centre of heel, between needle 1 and needle 4.

FOOT

Pick up 18 sts from side of heel flap with needle 1 and pick up 18 sts from other side of heel flap with needle 4 (81 sts). Start Fair Isle pattern starting at round 1 of chart B. Knit the sts picked up from the edge of the heel flap, turning sts knitwise.

Start gusset decrease: k2tog at end of needle 1, and ssk or skpo at beginning of needle 4 on the rounds as shown in chart B (rounds 2, 4, 6, 8, 10, 12, 14 and 16). The light grey squares on the chart represent places where there are no sts. After the gusset decrease there will be 65 sts (16–17–16–16).

Continue the Fair Isle pattern following the chart. On round 19 decrease 1 st at end of needle 4 (right sock) or beginning of needle 1 (left sock). When you have worked all 45 chart rounds, divide sts so that there are 16 sts on each needle. Work toe decreases following chart C. At the end of the toe, when there are 8 sts left, break off yarn and thread through remaining sts.

Weave in ends and steam block lightly.

CHART A1: RIGHT LEG

knit (in yarn B)

knit (in yarn A)

knit through back loop (in yarn A)

purl (in yarn A)

no st

next needle

CHART A2: LEFT LEG

knit (in yarn B)

knit (in yarn A)

knit through back loop (in yarn A)

purl (in yarn A)

no st

next needle

CHART B1: RIGHT FOOT

knit (in yarn B)

knit (in yarn A)

knit 2 together (in yarn A)

ssk: slip 2 sts knitwise one at a time onto RH needle, pass them back onto LH needle and knit thk to LH needle and knit them together through back loops (in yarn B)

no stitch

next needle

CHART B2: LEFT FOOT

CHART C1: RIGHT TOE DECREASE

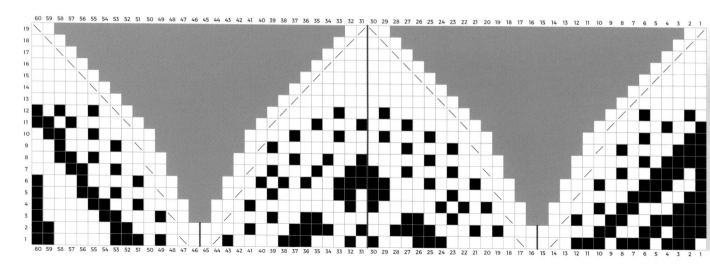

CHART C2: LEFT TOE DECREASE

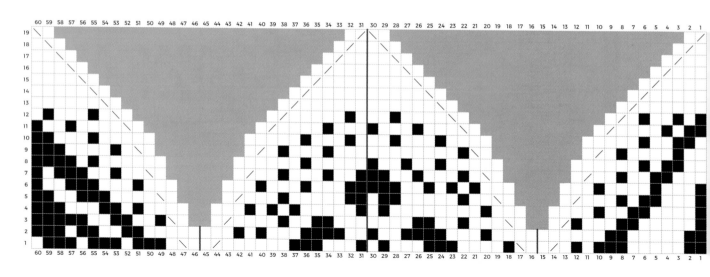

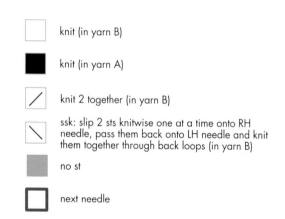

knit (in yarn B)

knit (in yarn A)

knit 2 together (in yarn B)

ssk: slip 2 sts knitwise one at a time onto RH needle, pass them back onto LH needle and knit them together through back loops (in yarn B)

no st

next needle

Enchanting

The secret of these socks is the lace design running down the back. The delicate, simple lace on the front of the sock and the tulip-inspired lace pattern on the back create an enchanting whole.

SIZES: UK 4 (Europe 37, US 6½) and UK 6 (Europe 39, US 8½); calf circumference: 33–38cm (13–15in)

YARN: 2 balls of Novita 7 Veljestä aran (10-ply/worsted) yarn in Peony 550; 100g/200m/218yd

AMOUNT USED: 150–160g (5¼–5¾oz)

KNITTING NEEDLES: 3.5mm (UK 9/10, US 4) DPN or size to obtain correct tension

TENSION (GAUGE): 21 sts and 26 rows/10cm (4in)

BEFORE YOU START

You can knit either size from the same written instructions. The instructions are identical until the end of the gusset decrease. After that the differences for the larger size are shown in blue.

In the charts for the leg, needles 1 and 2 form the back of the sock, and needles 3 and 4 form the front of the sock. After the heel, the needle numbering changes and needles 1 and 4 are used for the sole of the sock and needles 2 and 3 for the top.

LEG

Cast on 66 sts and divide between 4 needles as follows: 14–17–18–17. Join, being careful not to twist, and work in the round. Start working the leg from round 1 of chart A reading from right to left. On round 30 change the number of sts on each needle: 22–21–12–11. Decrease for the calf as indicated in the chart on rounds 31, 39, 43, 47, 51, 55, 59, 63 and 67. The decreases are shown on the chart on needles 1 and 2.

When you have worked all 98 rounds of the chart, divide sts between needles as follows: 13–12–12–11. Start the heel on needles 1 and 2 (25 sts) and leave the remaining sts on needles 3 and 4.

HEEL

Work the heel following chart B. Always slip the first st knitwise on RS and purlwise on WS. Work all 20 rounds of chart B.

Start to decrease to turn heel: work in st st. Starting with a RS row, knit until there are 8 sts left on LH needle. Decrease 1 st using ssk or skpo and turn work leaving 6 sts on the other needle. S1 purlwise and purl until 8 sts remain on LH needle. P2tog and turn work. Slip 1 and continue in st st until there are 7 sts left on LH needle. Decrease using ssk or skpo and turn work. S1 purlwise and purl until 7 sts remain on LH needle. P2tog and turn work. Continue in the same way, reducing the number of sts at the sides on each row and keeping the same number of sts (9) in the middle.

When you run out of side sts, divide the heel flap sts between 2 needles (5–4). K3, k2tog to bring yarn to centre of heel between needle 1 and needle 4.

FOOT

Pick up 11 sts from LH edge of heel flap using a spare needle. Knit the 4 sts from needle 1 and then the 11 picked up sts, turning sts knitwise. Work chart C pattern on needles 2 and 3 starting with chart round 1. Pick up and knit 11 sts from RH edge of heel flap, turning sts knitwise. Using the same needle, knit the 4 sts on needle 4 (53 sts).

Start gusset decrease: k2tog at end of needle 1, and ssk or skpo at beginning of needle 4 on every third round. Work in st st on needles 1 and 4 and work chart pattern on needles 2 and 3 repeating rounds 1–12. Continue decreasing gusset sts on every third round until there are 45 sts (11–12–11–11) – 47 sts (12–12–11–12).

Continue in st st on needles 1 and 4 and in chart pattern on needles 2 and 3. When you have worked 41 (44) rounds counted from the edge of the heel flap and have worked to the end of chart round 5 (8), start to decrease for the toe.

For the smaller size, work a wide wedge toe decrease to complete sock:
Needles 1 and 3: knit to last 3 sts, k2tog, k1.
Needles 2 and 4: k1, ssk, knit to end.
First work the decreases on every second round. Once there are 33 sts left (8–9–8–8), work the decreases on every round.

For the larger size, work a wide wedge toe decrease on needles 1 and 4. Work the toe decreases on needles 2 and 3 following chart D (rounds 1–4). After chart round 4, decrease following the instructions for a wide wedge toe decrease above on all needles on every round. On the last round miss out the decrease on needle 3.

When there are 9 (8) sts left, break off yarn and thread through remaining sts.

Weave in ends and steam block lightly.

KEY TO CHARTS A, C AND D

knit

knit through back loop

purl

knit 2 together

ssk: slip 2 sts knitwise one at a time onto RH needle, pass them back onto LH needle and knit them together through back loops

yarn over

slip 2 sts knitwise as if you were knitting them together, knit 1 st and pass the slipped sts over the knitted st

slip 1 st knitwise, knit 2 together and pass the slipped st over the knitted sts

place 1 st on cable needle and bring to front of work, k1 and k1 from cable needle

place 1 st on cable needle and bring to back of work, k1 and k1 from cable needle

no st

next needle

CHART A: LEG

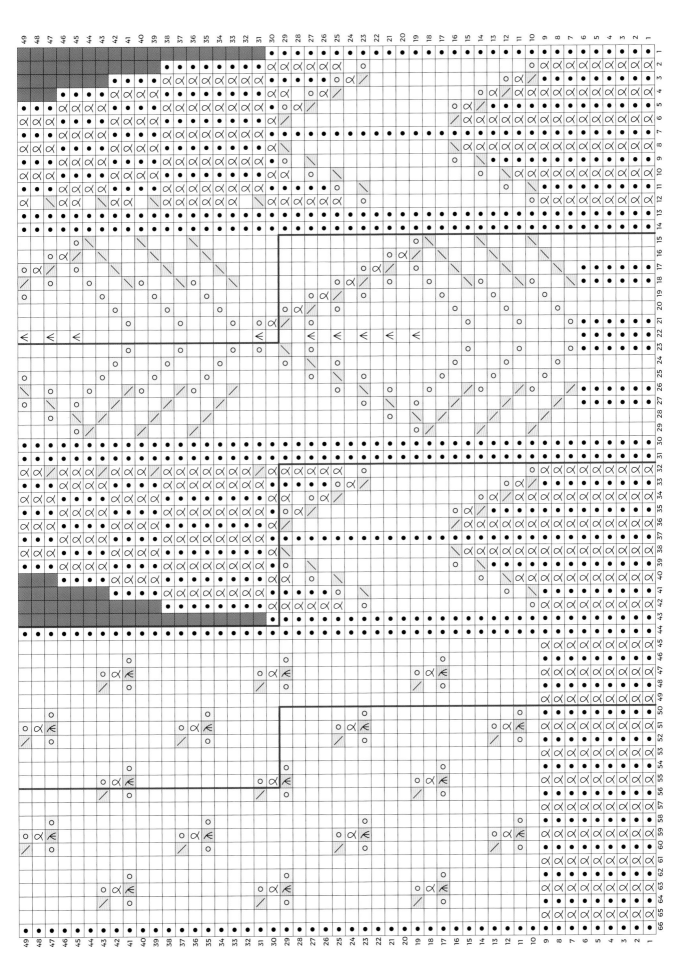

KEY TO CHART B

⬜	knit (RS), purl (WS)
Ω	knit through back loop (RS), purl through back loop (WS)
•	purl (WS), knit (RS)
\	ssk: slip 2 sts knitwise one at a time onto RH needle, pass them back onto LH needle and knit them together through back loops
/	knit 2 together
○	yarn over
⋀	slip 2 sts knitwise as if you were knitting them together, knit 1 st and pass the slipped sts over the knitted st
⋌	slip 1 st knitwise, knit 2 together and pass the slipped st over the knitted sts
⅄	increase 1 st: pick up the yarn between 2 sts in the previous round and knit through back loop
⊬	increase 1 st: pick up the yarn between 2 sts in the previous round and knit through front loop

CHART B: HEEL

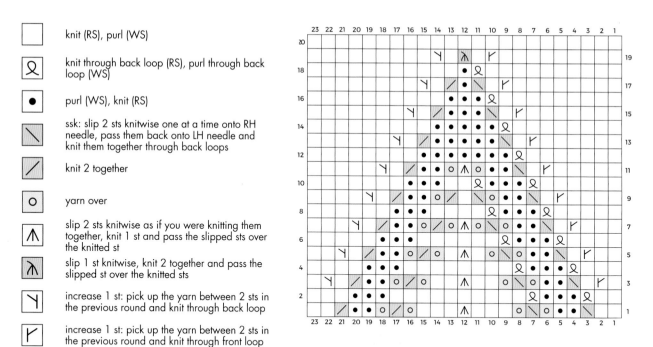

CHART C: FOOT

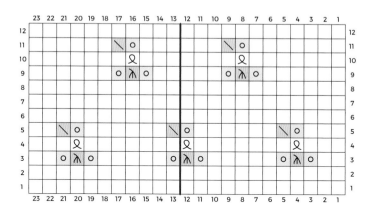

CHART D: TOE DECREASES (LARGER SIZE)

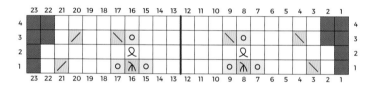

May

Marvel at new shoots, gaze at emerging buds of flowers and leaves and guess what each seedling is about to become. May is brimming with expectation and the light green of nature springing back into life.

SIZE: UK 6 (Europe 39, US 8½)

YARN: 2 balls of Novita Nalle DK (8-ply/light worsted) yarn in Nettle 366 (A) and 1 ball in Off-white 010 (B); 100g/260m/284yd

AMOUNT USED: 110g (3¾oz) A, 60g (2oz) B

KNITTING NEEDLES: 3mm (UK 11, US 2/3) or size to obtain correct tension

TENSION (GAUGE): 24 sts and 32 rows/ 10cm (4in)

BEFORE YOU START
The chart is read from bottom to top and from right to left. You can use 2.5mm (UK 12/13, US 1/2) or equivalent needles for the rib section to prevent the cuff from sagging.

If you want to make these socks for a larger calf size, change to 3.5mm (UK 9/10, US 4) needles for the Fair Isle pattern. This will produce socks for a calf circumference of more than 40cm (15¾in).

LEG

Cast on 75 sts in yarn A and divide between 4 needles as follows: 20–18–20–17. Join, being careful not to twist, and work in the round.

Start the rib pattern following the chart and work 13 rounds.

After the rib, start the Fair Isle pattern at chart round 14, increasing 1 st on the last needle on round 14 and dividing sts so you have 19 on each needle. Work leg following chart, decreasing in a suitable place at beginning of needle 1 and end of needle 4 on the following rounds:

Decrease on rounds: 45, 59, 76, 88, 95, 100, 105 and 110 (60 sts).
Note: on round 82 change the number of sts on each needle to 20–15–15–20.

When you have worked all 114 rounds for the leg, divide sts so there are 15 on each needle.

HEEL

Start heel flap in yarn A by knitting the sts on needle 1 onto needle 4 (30 sts for heel flap). Leave remaining sts on needles 2 and 3. Turn work, s1 purlwise and purl to end of row. Turn work.

Row 1 (RS): *s1, k1*, repeat from * to * to end of row. Turn work.
Row 2 (WS): s1 purlwise and purl to end of row. Turn work.
Repeat these two rows until heel flap has 30 rows and you have completed the last WS row.

Start to decrease to turn heel: continue in the same sl st pattern to reinforce heel. Starting with a RS row, knit until there are 11 sts left on the LH needle. Decrease 1 st using skpo and turn work leaving 9 sts on the other needle. S1 purlwise and purl until 11 sts remain on LH needle. P2tog and turn work. S1 knitwise and continue in sl st pattern until 10 sts remain on LH needle. Decrease using skpo and

turn work. S1 purlwise and purl until 10 sts remain on LH needle. P2tog and turn work. Continue in the same way, reducing the number of sts at the sides on each row and keeping the same number of sts (10) in the middle.

When you run out of side sts, divide the heel flap sts between 2 needles (5–5). K5 to bring yarn to centre of heel, between needle 1 and needle 4.

FOOT

Pick up 16 sts from LH edge of heel flap using a spare needle. Using yarn B, knit the 5 sts from needle 1 and then the 16 picked up sts, turning sts knitwise. Knit sts on needles 2 and 3. Pick up and knit 16 sts from RH edge of heel flap, turning sts knitwise. Using the same needle, knit the 5 sts on needle 4 (71 sts). The foot is worked in stripes: 2 rounds in yarn B, 2 rounds in yarn A.

Start gusset decrease: k2tog at end of needle 1, and ssk or skpo at beginning of needle 4 on every second round. Continue decreasing 2 gusset sts on every second round until there are 56 sts (14–14–14–14). Continue the foot in stripes in st st.

When you have worked 46 rounds counted from the edge of the heel flap, knit the remainder of the sock in yarn A, working a wide wedge toe:
Needles 1 and 3: knit to last 3 sts, k2tog, k1.
Needles 2 and 4: k1, ssk, knit to end.
Work this decrease on every second round until there are 10 sts left on each needle; then decrease on every round.
When there are 8 sts left, break off yarn and thread through remaining sts.

Weave in ends and steam block lightly.

	knit (in yarn A)		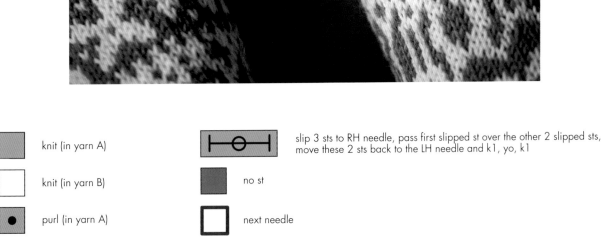	slip 3 sts to RH needle, pass first slipped st over the other 2 slipped sts, move these 2 sts back to the LH needle and k1, yo, k1
	knit (in yarn B)			no st
•	purl (in yarn A)			next needle

CHART: LEG

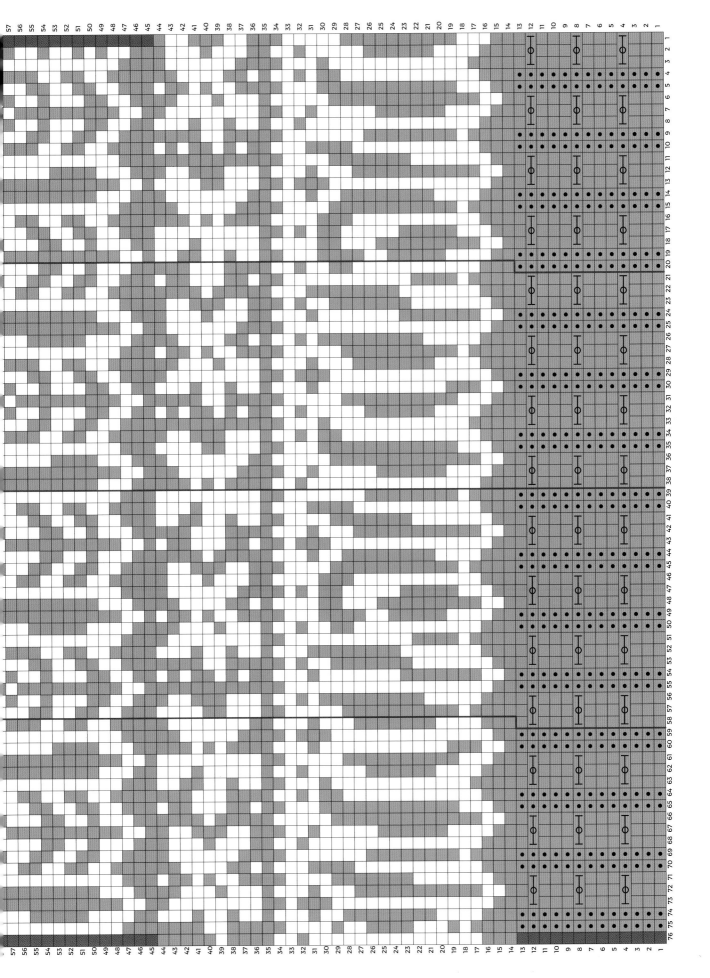

Happy Wanderer

These socks feature cable pathways, babbling streams and sparkling stories intertwined like spring garlands. Peering cautiously ahead, the happy wanderer breaks into a grin, looking forward to all the adventures of the approaching summer.

SIZE: UK 4 (Europe 37, US 6½) and UK 6 (Europe 39, US 8½)

YARN: 2 balls of Kaupunkilanka Kivijalka aran (10-ply/worsted) yarn in Orange 71; 100g/200m/218yd

AMOUNT USED: 105g–110g (3¾oz)

KNITTING NEEDLES: 3.5mm (UK 9/10, US 4) DPN or size to obtain correct tension and two cable needles

TENSION (GAUGE): 21 sts and 24 rows/ 10cm (4in)

BEFORE YOU START

Both sizes are shown on chart A for the leg pattern; the smaller size is shown between the blue lines while the larger size uses the whole width of the chart. You can knit either size from the same written instructions.

The differences for the larger size are shown in blue. If you can try on the sock as you go, start the toe decrease when the foot of the sock reaches the top of the little toe.

LEG

Cast on 47 (51) sts and divide between 4 needles as follows: 11–13–12–11 (13–13–12–13). Join, being careful not to twist, and work in the round. Work all of chart A (52 rounds).

HEEL

Start reinforced heel flap by knitting the sts on needle 1 onto needle 4 (22 (26) sts for heel flap). Leave remaining sts on needles 2 and 3. Turn work, s1 purlwise and purl to end of row. For the smaller size, increase 2 sts at the same time (24 sts). For the larger size, decrease 2 sts at the same time (24 sts). Turn work.

Row 1 (RS): *s1, k1*, repeat from * to * to end of row. Turn work.
Row 2 (WS): s1 purlwise and purl to end of row. Turn work.
Repeat these two rows until heel flap has 24 rows and you have completed the last WS row.

Start to decrease to turn heel: continue in the same sl st pattern to reinforce heel. Starting with a RS row, knit until there are 9 sts left on LH needle. Decrease 1 st using ssk or skpo and turn work leaving 7 sts on the other needle. S1 purlwise and purl until 9 sts remain on LH needle. P2tog and turn work. Slip 1 knitwise and continue in sl st pattern until there are 8 sts left on LH needle. Decrease using ssk or skpo and turn work. S1 purlwise and purl until 8 sts remain on LH needle. P2tog and turn work. Continue in the same way, reducing the number of sts at the sides on each row and keeping the same number of sts (8) in the middle.

When you run out of side sts, divide the heel flap sts between 2 needles (4–4). K4 to bring yarn to centre of heel, between needle 1 and needle 4.

FOOT

Pick up 14 sts from LH edge of heel flap using a spare needle. Knit the 4 sts from needle 1 and then the 14 picked up sts, turning sts knitwise. Work chart B on needles 2 and 3 starting with chart round 1. Pick up and knit 14 sts from RH edge of heel flap turning sts knitwise. Using the same needle, knit the 4 sts on needle 4 (61 sts).

Start gusset decrease: k2tog at end of needle 1, and ssk or skpo at beginning of needle 4 on every second round. Work in st st on needles 1 and 4 and chart pattern on needles 2 and 3 repeating chart rounds 1–12. Continue decreasing 2 gusset sts on every second round until there are 47 sts (11–13–12–11) – 49 sts (12–13–12–12).
Continue in st st on needles 1 and 4 and in chart pattern on needles 2 and 3 to the end of chart B. Then continue in st st on all needles.

When you have knitted 42 rounds (46 rounds) after the heel flap, divide sts on needles as follows: 12–12–11–12 (12–13–12–12) and end sock with a wide wedge toe:
Needles 1 and 3: knit to last 3 sts, k2tog, k1.
Needles 2 and 4: k1, ssk, knit to end.
First work the decreases on every second round. Once there are 31 sts left (8–8–7–8) – 33 sts (8–9–8–8), work the decreases on every round. For smaller size: on the last round miss out the decrease on needle 3. When there are 8 sts (9 sts) left, break off yarn and thread through remaining sts.

Weave in ends and steam block lightly.

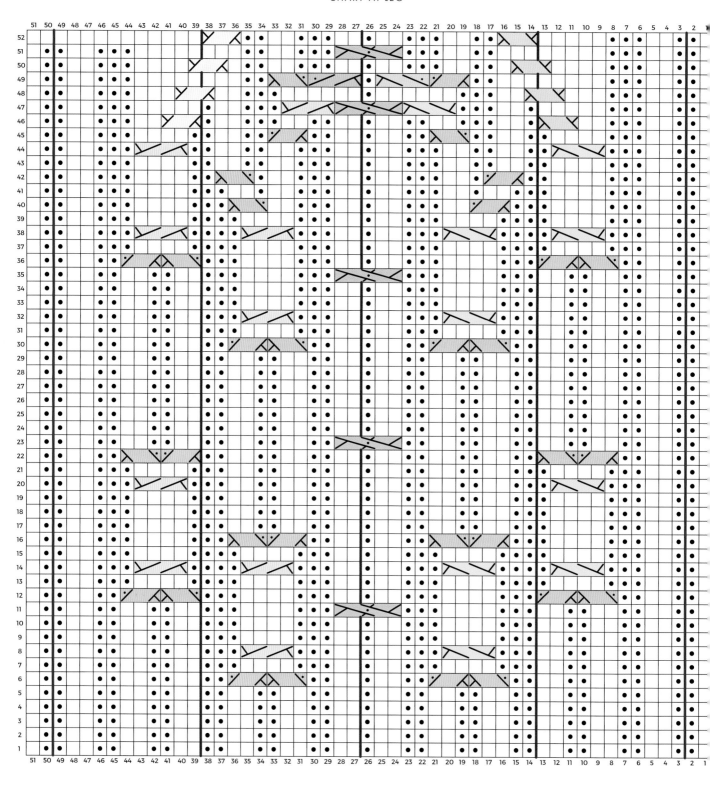

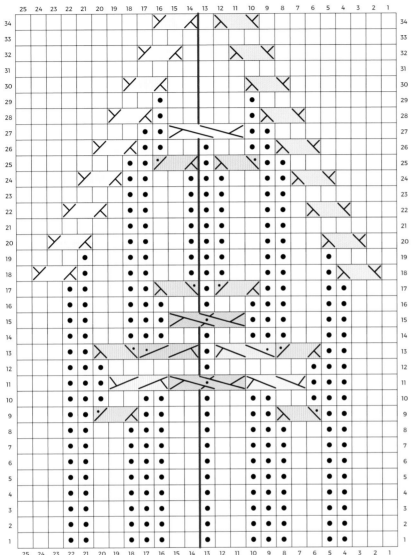

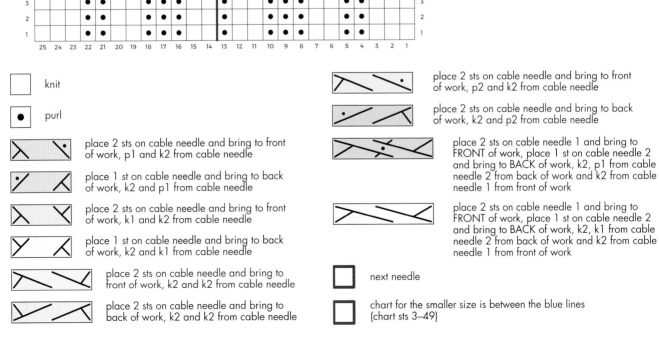

knit

• purl

place 2 sts on cable needle and bring to front of work, p1 and k2 from cable needle

place 1 st on cable needle and bring to back of work, k2 and p1 from cable needle

place 2 sts on cable needle and bring to front of work, k1 and k2 from cable needle

place 1 st on cable needle and bring to back of work, k2 and k1 from cable needle

place 2 sts on cable needle and bring to front of work, k2 and k2 from cable needle

place 2 sts on cable needle and bring to back of work, k2 and k2 from cable needle

place 2 sts on cable needle and bring to front of work, p2 and k2 from cable needle

place 2 sts on cable needle and bring to back of work, k2 and p2 from cable needle

place 2 sts on cable needle 1 and bring to FRONT of work, place 1 st on cable needle 2 and bring to BACK of work, k2, p1 from cable needle 2 from back of work and k2 from cable needle 1 from front of work

place 2 sts on cable needle 1 and bring to FRONT of work, place 1 st on cable needle 2 and bring to BACK of work, k2, k1 from cable needle 2 from back of work and k2 from cable needle 1 from front of work

next needle

chart for the smaller size is between the blue lines (chart sts 3–49)

SUMMER

summer

Dear Sister

These socks are for my sisters, who share in my happiness and sorrows. The fluttering butterflies and the exuberant colour palette encapsulate the joys of siblings; shared encounters, sociable evenings and endless laughter under the midnight sun. This pattern is more challenging than usual, but it's wonderfully rewarding.

SIZE: UK 6 (Europe 39, US 8½)

YARN: 2 balls of Drops Fabel 4-ply (fingering) yarn in Off-white 100 (A); 50g/205m/224yd
1 ball of Scheepjes Invicta Colour 4-ply (fingering) in 963 (B); 100g/420m/459yds, **or** 1 ball of Nordlys Viking 4-ply (fingering) in 956 (B); 100g/350m/383yds

AMOUNT USED: 100g (3½oz) A, 50g (1¾oz) B

KNITTING NEEDLES: 2.5mm (UK 12/13, US 1/2) DPN or size to obtain correct tension

TENSION (GAUGE): 31 sts and 33 rows/ 10cm (4in)

LEG

Cast on 84 sts in yarn A and divide between 4 needles with 21 sts on each needle. Join, being careful not to twist, and work in the round.

Start in twisted rib following chart A and knit 13 rounds in rib.

After the rib, start the Fair Isle pattern at chart round 14. Divide sts between needles as follows: 21–22–20–21. Work leg following chart, decreasing at beginning of needle 1 and end of needle 4 on the rounds as shown at the top of the next page:

Decrease on rounds: 34, 43, 49, 57, 63, 68, 72, 76, 80 and 84 (64 sts).

Note: on round 61 change the number of sts on each needle to 22–17–16–21.

If the leg feels tight, do not work the last decreases and decrease the extra sts on the first row of the heel flap instead.

When you have worked all 104 rounds for the leg, divide sts between needles as follows: 16–17–16–15.

HEEL

Start heel flap in yarn A by knitting the sts on needle 1 onto needle 4 (31 sts for heel flap). Leave remaining sts on needles 2 and 3. Turn work, s1 purlwise and purl to end of row. At the same time, increase 1 st (32 sts). Turn work.

Row 1 (RS): *s1, k1*, repeat from * to * to end of row. Turn work.
Row 2 (WS): s1 purlwise and purl to end of row. Turn work.
Repeat these two rows until heel flap has 32 rows and you have completed the last WS row.

Start to decrease to turn heel: continue in the same sl st pattern to reinforce heel. Starting with a RS row, knit until there are 11 sts left on LH needle. Decrease 1 st using skpo and turn work, leaving 9 sts on the other needle. S1 purlwise and purl until 11 sts remain on LH needle. P2tog and turn work. S1 and continue in sl st pattern until there are 10 sts left on LH needle. Decrease using ssk or skpo and turn work. S1 purlwise and purl until 10 sts remain on LH needle. P2tog and turn work. Continue in the same way, reducing the number of sts at the sides on each row and keeping the same number of sts (12) in the middle.

When you run out of side sts, divide the heel flap sts between 2 needles (6–6). K6 to bring yarn to centre of heel, between needle 1 and needle 4.

FOOT

Pick up 18 sts from side of heel flap with needle 1 and pick up 18 sts from other side of heel flap with needle 4 (81 sts).

Start Fair Isle pattern starting at round 1 of chart B. Knit the sts picked up from the edge of the heel flap, turning sts knitwise.

Start gusset decrease: k2tog at end of needle 1, and ssk or skpo at beginning of needle 4 on rounds as shown in chart B (rounds 2, 3, 5, 6, 8, 9, 11 and 12). The grey squares on the chart represent places where there are no sts. After the gusset decrease there will be 65 sts (16–17–16–16).

Continue in Fair Isle pattern following chart (46 rounds). On last round, decrease 1 st at end of needle 4 and divide sts so there are 16 sts on each needle.

Finish sock in yarn A, working a wide wedge toe:
Needles 1 and 3: knit to last 3 sts, k2tog, k1.
Needles 2 and 4: k1, ssk or skpo, knit to end.
First work the decreases on every second round. Once there are 11 sts left, work decreases on every round. When there are 8 sts left, break off yarn and thread through remaining sts.

Weave in ends and steam block lightly.

CHART A: LEG

knit (in yarn A)

knit (in yarn B)

• purl

⊢⊣ twisted rib: slip 1 st to RH needle, knit next st first through front loop and then through back loop, pass slipped st over knitted sts

⟋ knit 2 together (in yarn A)

⟍ ssk: slip 2 sts knitwise one at a time onto RH needle, pass them back onto LH needle and knit them together through back loops (in yarn A)

⟋ knit 2 together (in yarn B)

⟍ ssk: slip 2 sts knitwise one at a time onto RH needle, pass them back onto LH needle and knit them together through back loops (in yarn B)

no st

next needle

knit (in yarn A)

knit (in yarn B)

● purl

⊢⊣ twisted rib: slip 1 st to RH needle, knit next st first through front loop and then through back loop, pass slipped st over knitted sts

/ knit 2 together (in yarn A)

\ ssk: slip 2 sts knitwise one at a time onto RH needle, pass them back onto LH needle and knit them together through back loops (in yarn A)

/ knit 2 together (in yarn B)

\ ssk: slip 2 sts knitwise one at a time onto RH needle, pass them back onto LH needle and knit them together through back loops (in yarn B)

no st

next needle

Careless Love

Carefree moments lying on the grass, whispering in the shade of the trees. Gentle breezes and picnics, tenderness and silliness on summer nights, kisses behind the barn. These socks are full of utterly intoxicating, foolish love. Memories you never want to forget.

SIZE: UK 5/6 (Europe 38/39, US 7½/8½)

YARN: 1 ball of Malabrigo Sock 3-ply (fingering) yarn in Fucsia 093; 100g/402m/439yd, **or** 1 ball of Louhittaren Luola Väinämöinen 4-ply (fingering) in Fuchsia; 100g/400m/437yd

AMOUNT USED: 60g (2oz)

KNITTING NEEDLES: 2.5mm (UK 12/13, US 1/2) DPN or size to obtain correct tension and two cable needles

TENSION (GAUGE): 28 sts and 36 rows/ 10cm (4in)

BEFORE YOU START

The right and left socks are mirror images of each other. The legs of both socks are knitted from the same chart but for the foot use chart B Right for the right sock and chart B Left for the left sock. Otherwise, the instructions are the same for both socks.

LEG

Cast on 64 sts and divide between 4 needles as follows: 15–15–16–18. Join, being careful not to twist, and work in the round. Work leg following chart A (52 rounds).

HEEL

Start reinforced heel flap by knitting the sts on needle 1 onto needle 4 (33 sts for heel flap). Leave remaining sts on needles 2 and 3. Turn work, s1 purlwise and purl to end of row. At the same time, decrease 1 st making 32 sts for heel flap. Turn work.

Row 1 (RS): *s1, k1*, repeat from * to * to end of row. Turn work.
Row 2 (WS): s1 purlwise and purl to end of row. Turn work.
Repeat these two rows until heel flap has 32 rows and you have completed the last WS row.

Start to decrease to turn heel: continue in the same sl st pattern to reinforce heel. Starting with a RS row, knit until there are 11 sts left on LH needle. Decrease 1 st using ssk or skpo and turn work leaving 9 sts on the other needle. S1 purlwise and purl until 11 sts remain on LH needle. P2tog and turn work. S1 and continue in sl st pattern until there are 10 sts left on LH needle. Decrease using ssk or skpo and turn work. S1 purlwise and purl until 10 sts remain on LH needle. P2tog and turn work. Continue in the same way, reducing the number of sts at the sides on each row and keeping the same number of sts (12) in the middle.

When you run out of side sts, divide the heel flap sts between 2 needles (6–6). K6 to bring yarn to centre of heel, between needle 1 and needle 4.

FOOT

Pick up 18 sts from LH edge of heel flap using a spare needle. Knit the 6 sts from needle 1 and then the 18 picked up sts, turning sts knitwise. Work chart B pattern on needles 2 and 3 starting with chart round 1. Pick up and knit 18 sts from RH edge of heel flap turning sts knitwise. Using the same needle, knit the 6 sts on needle 4 (79 sts).

Start gusset decrease: k2tog at end of needle 1, and ssk or skpo at beginning of needle 4 on every second round. Continue following chart B on needles 2 and 3. Continue decreasing 2 gusset sts on every second round until there are 63 sts (16–15–16–16). Continue in st st on needles 1 and 4 and in chart pattern on needles 2 and 3 to the end of chart B. Then continue in st st on all needles.

When you have knitted 60 rounds after the heel flap, end sock with a wide wedge toe:
Needles 1 and 3: knit to last 3 sts, k2tog, k1.
Needles 2 and 4: k1, ssk, knit to end.
First work the decreases on every second round. Once there are 39 sts left (10–9–10–10), work the decreases on every round. When there are 11 sts left, break off yarn and thread through remaining sts.

Weave in ends and steam block lightly.

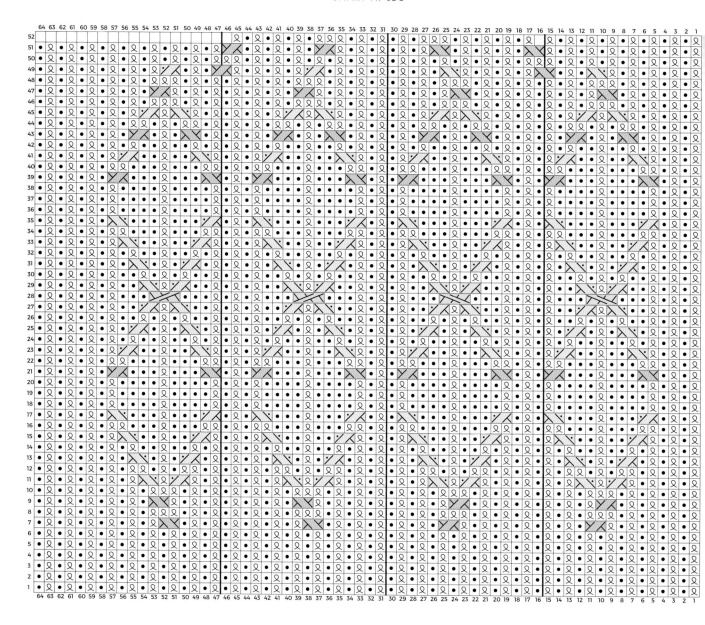

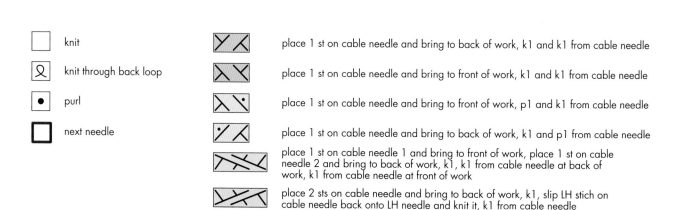

	knit
	knit through back loop
	purl
	next needle

place 1 st on cable needle and bring to back of work, k1 and k1 from cable needle

place 1 st on cable needle and bring to front of work, k1 and k1 from cable needle

place 1 st on cable needle and bring to front of work, p1 and k1 from cable needle

place 1 st on cable needle and bring to back of work, k1 and p1 from cable needle

place 1 st on cable needle 1 and bring to front of work, place 1 st on cable needle 2 and bring to back of work, k1, k1 from cable needle at back of work, k1 from cable needle at front of work

place 2 sts on cable needle and bring to back of work, k1, slip LH stich on cable needle back onto LH needle and knit it, k1 from cable needle

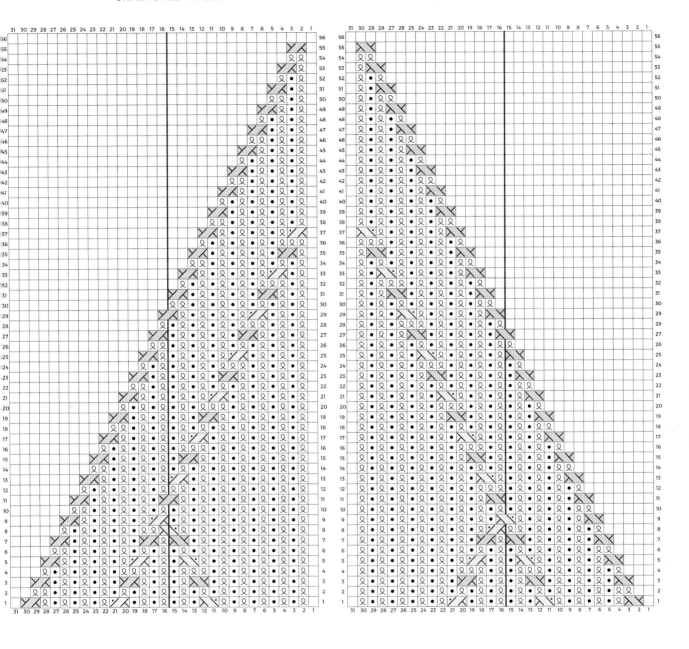

Hair of Gold

*The yellow gold of summer, flower crowns in your hair,
sunny days and smiley, dimpled faces eating ice cream.
These short socks are made for hot summer days and
knit up quickly for a warm day in July.*

SIZES: UK 4 (Europe 37, US 6½) and UK 6 (Europe 39, US 8½)

YARN: 1 (2) balls of Teetee Pallas DK (8-ply/light worsted) yarn in Yellow 26; 50g/130m/142yd

AMOUNT USED: 50g (1¾oz)–55g (2oz)

KNITTING NEEDLES: 3mm (UK 11, US 2/3) DPN or size to obtain correct tension

TENSION (GAUGE): 23 sts and 28 rows/10cm (4in)

BEFORE YOU START

You can knit either size from the same written instructions. The instructions are identical until the end of the gusset decrease. After that the differences for the larger size are shown in blue.

The abbreviation TBL means through back loop.

LEG

Cast on 54 sts and divide between 4 needles as follows: 14–14–13–13. Join, being careful not to twist, and work in the round. Work in rib, k1 TBL, p1 for 10 rounds.

HEEL

Start reinforced heel flap by knitting the sts on needle 1 onto needle 4 continuing the rib pattern (27 sts). Leave remaining sts on needles 2 and 3. Turn work and s1 purlwise, p1, *k1, s1 with yarn in front*, repeat from * to * until last 2 sts, p2. Turn work.

Row 1 (RS): s1, *k1 TBL, p1*, repeat from * to * until last 2 sts, k1 TBL, k1. Turn work.
Row 2 (WS): s1 purlwise, p1, *k1, s1 with yarn in front*, repeat from * to * until last 2 sts, p2. Turn work.
Repeat these two rows until heel flap has 28 rows and you have completed the last WS row.

Start to decrease to turn heel: continue in the same rib pattern to reinforce heel. Starting with a RS row, knit until there are 9 sts left on LH needle. Decrease 1 st using ssk or skpo and turn work leaving 7 sts on the other needle. S1 purlwise, and continue in rib pattern until 9 sts remain on LH needle. P2tog and turn work. S1 and continue in rib pattern until there are 8 sts left on LH needle. Decrease using ssk or skpo and turn work. S1 purlwise, and continue in rib pattern until 8 sts remain on LH needle. P2tog and turn work. Continue in the same way, reducing the number of sts at the sides on each row and keeping the same number of sts (11) in the middle.

When you run out of side sts, divide the heel flap sts between 2 needles (6–5). K4, k2tog to bring yarn to centre of heel between needle 1 and needle 4.

FOOT

Pick up 16 sts from LH edge of heel flap using a spare needle. Knit the 5 sts from needle 1 and then the 16 picked up sts, turning sts knitwise. Work chart pattern on needles 2 and 3 starting with chart round 1. At the same time, increase 1 st on needle 3. Pick up and knit 16 sts from RH edge of heel flap turning sts knitwise. Using the same needle, knit the 5 sts on needle 4 (70 sts).

Start gusset decrease: k2tog at end of needle 1, and ssk or skpo at beginning of needle 4 on every second round. Continue following chart B on needles 2 and 3 and repeating rounds 1–11. Continue decreasing 2 gusset sts on every second round until there are 52 sts (12–14–14–12) – 56 sts (14–14–14–14).

Continue in st st on needles 1 and 4 and in chart pattern on needles 2 and 3. When you have worked 44 (49) rounds counted from the edge of the heel flap and have completed round 11 (5) of the chart, work one more round and for the smaller size divide sts so there are 13 on each needle.

Finish sock with a wide wedge toe:
Needle 1: knit to last 3 sts, k2tog, k1.
Needle 2: ssk, knit to end.
Needle 3: knit to last 2 sts, k2tog.
Needle 4: k1, ssk, knit to end.
First work the decreases on every second round. Once there are 32 sts left (8–8–8–8), work the decreases on every round. When there are 8 sts left, break off yarn and thread through remaining sts.

Weave in ends and steam block lightly.

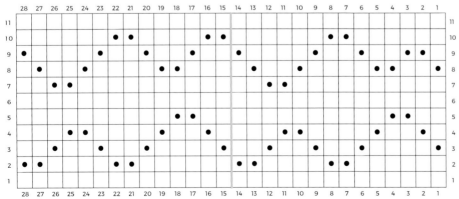

Paradise

A green paradise, lush and leafy with the scent of fresh grass. In a maze of lacework, find forest trails, the charm of summer flowers and a sense of the lighter nights slowly drawing in.

SIZE: UK 5/6 (Europe 38/39, US 7½/8½)

YARN: 1 ball of Kirjo-Pirkka 4-ply (fingering) yarn in Lime 49; 100g/420m/459yd

AMOUNT USED: 52g (1¾oz)

KNITTING NEEDLES: 2.5mm (UK 12/13, US 1/2) DPN or size to obtain correct tension

TENSION (GAUGE): 28 sts and 36 rows/ 10cm (4in)

LEG

Cast on 65 sts and divide between 4 needles as follows: 16–16–15–18. Join, being careful not to twist, and work in the round.

Work rounds 1–35 of leg as follows:
Needle 1: k2, p2, k2, p2, k2, p2, k2, p2.
Needles 2 and 3: work rounds 1–35 of chart A in pattern.
Needle 4: p2, k2, p2, k2, p2, k2, p2, k2, p2.

On last round of leg, work sts on needle 4 in st st instead of rib.

HEEL

Start decorative reinforced heel flap by knitting the sts on needle 1 onto needle 4 (34 sts for heel flap). Leave remaining sts on needles 2 and 3. Turn work, s1 purlwise and purl to end of row. At the same time, decrease 2 sts making 32 sts for heel flap. Turn work.

Row 1 (RS): *s1, k1*, repeat from * to * to end of row. Turn work.
Row 2 (WS): s1 purlwise and purl to end of row. Turn work.
Row 3 (RS): s1, k1, *k1, s1*, repeat from * to * to last 2 sts, k2. Turn work.
Row 4 (WS): s1 purlwise and purl to end of row. Turn work.
Repeat these four rows until the heel flap has 32 rows and you have completed the last row 4.

Start to decrease to turn heel: continue in the same sl st pattern to reinforce heel. Starting with a RS row, knit until there are 11 sts left on LH needle. Decrease 1 st using ssk or skpo and turn work leaving 9 sts on the other needle. S1 purlwise and purl until 11 sts remain on LH needle. P2tog and turn work. S1 and continue in sl st pattern until there are 10 sts left on LH needle. Decrease using ssk or skpo and turn work. S1 purlwise and purl until 10 sts remain on LH needle. P2tog and turn work. Continue in the same way, reducing the number of sts at the sides on each row and keeping the same number of sts (12) in the middle.

When you run out of side sts, divide the heel flap sts between 2 needles (6–6). K6 to bring yarn to centre of heel, between needle 1 and needle 4.

FOOT

Pick up 18 sts from LH edge of heel flap using a spare needle. Knit the 6 sts from needle 1 and then the 18 picked up sts, turning sts knitwise. Work chart B pattern on needles 2 and 3 starting with chart round 1 and repeating chart rounds 1–30. Pick up and knit 18 sts from RH edge of heel flap turning sts knitwise. Using the same needle, knit the 6 sts on needle 4 (79 sts).

Start gusset decrease: k2tog at end of needle 1, and ssk or skpo at beginning of needle 4 on every second round. Continue following chart B on needles 2 and 3. Continue decreasing 2 gusset sts on every second round until there are 63 sts (16–16–15–16). Continue in st st on needles 1 and 4 and in chart pattern on needles 2 and 3. When you have knitted 60 rounds after the heel flap, start to decrease for the toe.

Work a wide wedge toe decrease on needles 1 and 4 and follow chart pattern (with toe decreases) on needles 2 and 3.
Needle 1: knit to last 3 sts, k2tog, k1.
Needle 4: k1, ssk, knit to end.
Work this decrease on every second round until there are 9 sts left on each needle. Then decrease on every round.
Needles 2 and 3: work toe decreases following chart C (rounds 1–19).
Work until 11 sts remain. Break off yarn and thread through remaining sts.

Weave in ends and steam block lightly.

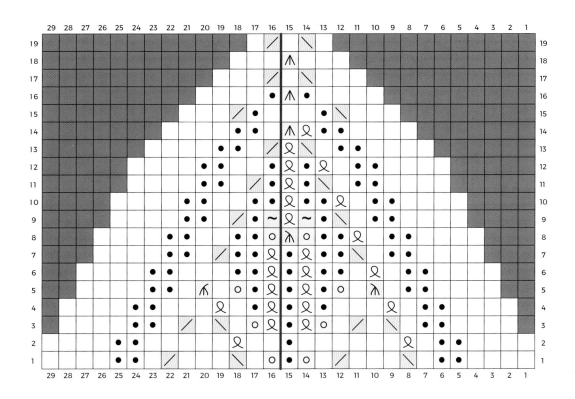

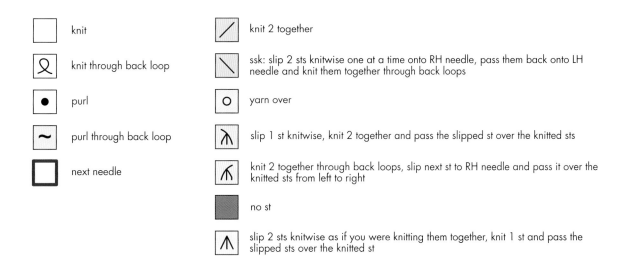

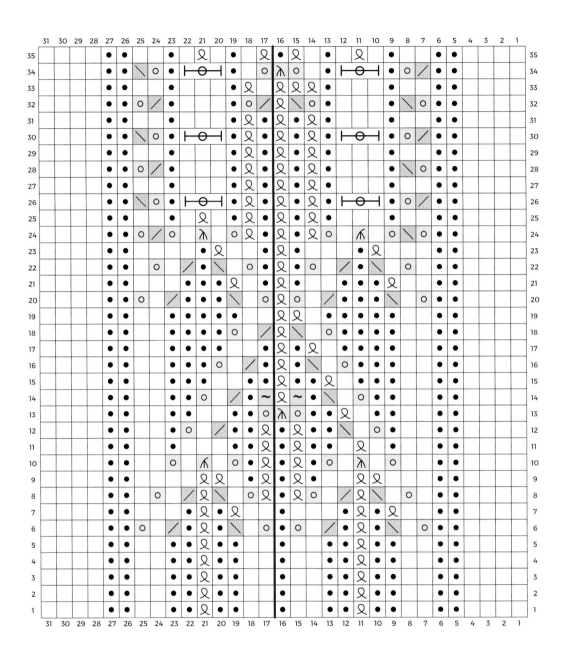

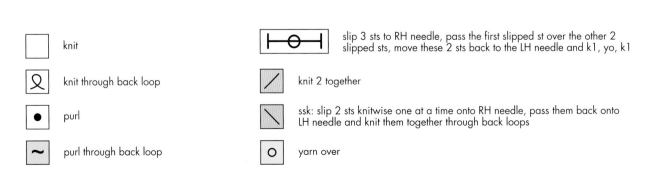

☐	knit
Ⴔ	knit through back loop
•	purl
~	purl through back loop
⊢O⊣	slip 3 sts to RH needle, pass the first slipped st over the other 2 slipped sts, move these 2 sts back to the LH needle and k1, yo, k1
/	knit 2 together
\	ssk: slip 2 sts knitwise one at a time onto RH needle, pass them back onto LH needle and knit them together through back loops
O	yarn over

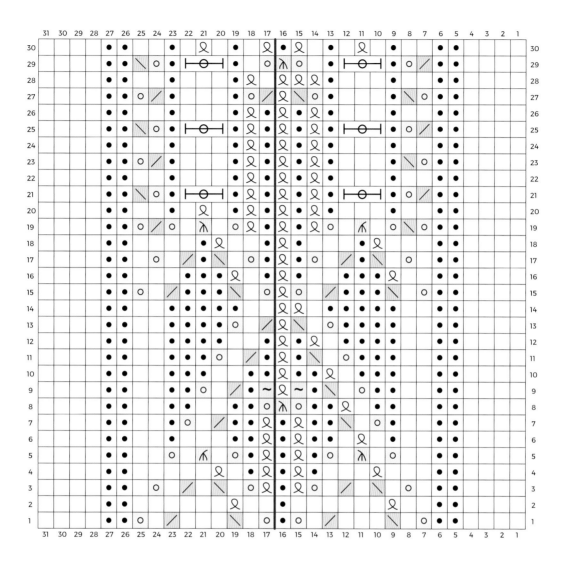

slip 1 st knitwise, knit 2 together and pass the slipped st over the knitted sts

knit 2 together through back loops, slip next st to RH needle and pass it over the knitted sts from left to right

slip 2 sts knitwise as if you were knitting them together, knit 1 st and pass the slipped sts over the knitted st

next needle

Wedding Waltz

*The whirl of a summer wedding; an enchanting night, glowing
with love. These socks epitomize the spirit of a waltz in the
middle of an August night as cables entwine like two beautiful
lovers together at last. The final celebration of the summer.
Lock its stories away in your heart and step towards a new,
wonderful autumn.*

SIZE: UK 5/6 (Europe 38/39, US 7½/8½)

YARN: 1 ball of Kaupunkilanka Rotvalli DK
(8-ply/light worsted) in White 01 (A) and 1 ball in
Dark Grey 95 (B); 100g/260m/284yd

AMOUNT USED: 60g (2oz) A, 60g (2oz) B

KNITTING NEEDLES: 3mm (UK 11, US 2/3)
DPN or size to obtain correct tension, cable needle

TENSION (GAUGE): 26 sts and 32 rows/
10cm (4in)

BEFORE YOU START
Charts are read from bottom to top and from right to
left. The combination of cables with Fair Isle can make
for a tighter leg. If possible, try the sock on at the very
start and switch to larger needles if necessary.

LEG

Cast on 59 sts in yarn B. Divide between 4 needles as follows: 14–16–15–14. Join, being careful not to twist, and work in the round. Start leg following chart A and work rounds 1–8. Work chart round 9 in st st, increasing 4 sts at the same time. Check that sts are divided between needles as follows: 16–16–15–16 Start the Fair Isle pattern from round 10 of chart A and work leg as shown on chart.

HEEL

When you have worked all 42 chart rounds for the leg, start the reinforced heel flap in yarn A by knitting the sts on needle 1 onto needle 4 (32 sts). Leave remaining sts on needles 2 and 3. Turn work, s1 purlwise and purl to end of row. At the same time, decrease 2 sts making 30 sts for heel flap. Turn work.

Row 1 (RS): *s1, k1*, repeat from * to * to end of row. Turn work.
Row 2 (WS): s1 purlwise and purl to end of row. Turn work.
Repeat these two rows until heel flap has 30 rows and you have completed the last WS row.

Start to decrease to turn heel: starting with a RS row, work in reinforced sl st pattern until there are 11 sts left on the LH needle. Decrease 1 st using skpo and turn work leaving 9 sts on the other needle. S1 purlwise and purl until 11 sts remain on LH needle. P2tog and turn work. S1 and continue in sl st pattern until 10 sts remain on LH needle. Decrease using skpo and turn work. S1 purlwise and purl until 10 sts remain on LH needle. P2tog and turn work. Continue in the same way, reducing the number of sts at the sides on each row and keeping the same number of sts (10) in the middle.

When you run out of side sts, divide the heel flap sts between 2 needles (5–5). K5 to bring yarn to centre of heel, between needle 1 and needle 4.

FOOT

Pick up 17 sts from side of heel flap with needle 1 and pick up 17 sts from other side of heel flap with needle 4 (75 sts). Continue Fair Isle pattern starting from round 1 of chart B. Knit the sts picked up from the edge of the heel flap, turning sts knitwise.

Start gusset decrease: k2tog at end of needle 1 and ssk or skpo at beginning of needle 4 on rounds as shown in chart B (rounds 2, 4, 6, 8, 10 and 12). The dark grey squares on the chart represent places where there are no sts. After the gusset decrease there will be 61 sts (15–16–15–15). Continue the Fair Isle pattern following the chart.

When you have worked all 42 rows of chart B, finish sock with a wide wedge toe in yarn A.
Needles 1 and 3: knit to last 3 sts, k2tog, k1.
Needles 2 and 4: k1, ssk or skpo, knit to end.
Work the decreases on every second round. Once there are 41 sts left (10–11–10–10), work decreases on every round. When there are 9 sts left, break off yarn and thread through remaining sts.

Weave in ends and steam block lightly.

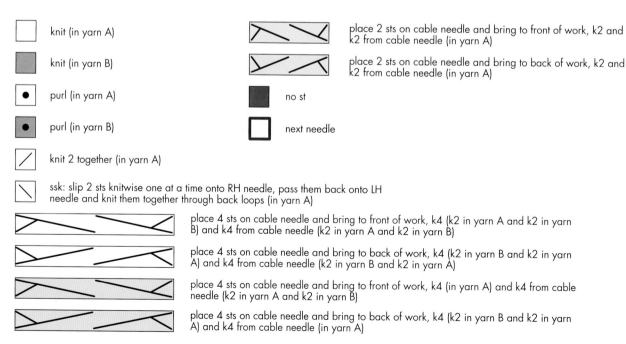

	knit (in yarn A)			place 2 sts on cable needle and bring to front of work, k2 and k2 from cable needle (in yarn A)
	knit (in yarn B)			place 2 sts on cable needle and bring to back of work, k2 and k2 from cable needle (in yarn A)
•	purl (in yarn A)			no st
•	purl (in yarn B)			next needle
/	knit 2 together (in yarn A)			
\	ssk: slip 2 sts knitwise one at a time onto RH needle, pass them back onto LH needle and knit them together through back loops (in yarn A)			

place 4 sts on cable needle and bring to front of work, k4 (k2 in yarn A and k2 in yarn B) and k4 from cable needle (k2 in yarn A and k2 in yarn B)

place 4 sts on cable needle and bring to back of work, k4 (k2 in yarn B and k2 in yarn A) and k4 from cable needle (k2 in yarn B and k2 in yarn A)

place 4 sts on cable needle and bring to front of work, k4 (in yarn A) and k4 from cable needle (k2 in yarn A and k2 in yarn B)

place 4 sts on cable needle and bring to back of work, k4 (k2 in yarn B and k2 in yarn A) and k4 from cable needle (in yarn A)

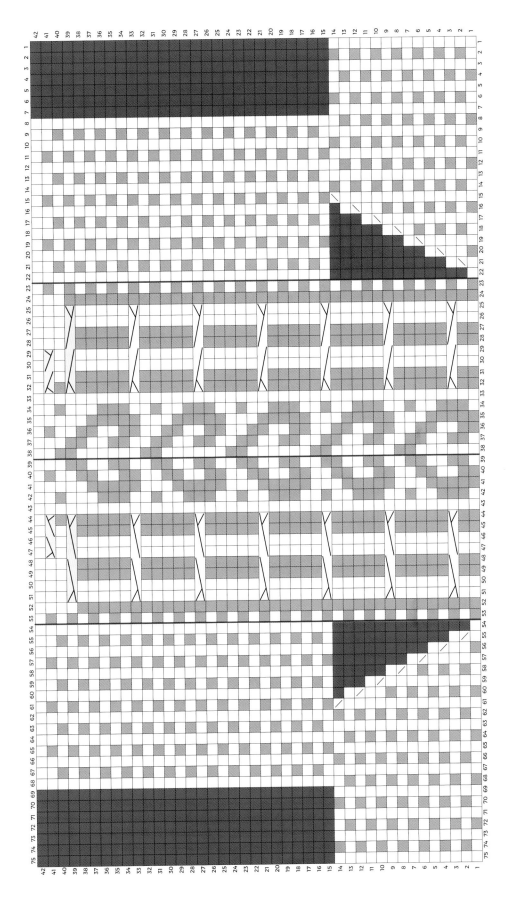

AUTUMN

Endless

Stealthily, as if on tiptoe, endless summer seamlessly merges into autumn. Wandering through autumnal forests, and clasping hands, drinking in the dark scent of the spruce trees in the mist.

SIZE: UK 5/6 (Europe 38/39, US 7½/8½)

YARN: 4 balls of Gjestal Maija DK (8-ply/ light worsted) yarn in Forest Green 212; 50g/130m/142yd

AMOUNT USED: 160g (5¾oz)

KNITTING NEEDLES: 3mm (UK 11, US 2/3) DPN or size to obtain correct tension

TENSION (GAUGE): 24 sts and 30 rows/ 10cm (4in)

LEG

Cast on 74 sts and divide between 4 needles as follows: 19–18–17–20. Join, being careful not to twist, and work in the round. The number of sts per needle varies on the chart due to the increases and decreases. Work all 116 rounds of chart A. Due to the decreases for the calf, you will have 57 sts by the end. Before starting the heel, divide them between the needles as follows: 14–15–14–14.

HEEL

Start reinforced heel flap by knitting the sts on needle 1 onto needle 4 (28 sts for heel flap). Leave remaining sts on needles 2 and 3. Turn work, s1 purlwise and purl to end of row. Turn work.

Row 1 (RS): *s1, k1*, repeat from * to * to end of row. Turn work.
Row 2 (WS): s1 purlwise and purl to end of row.
Repeat these two rows until heel flap has 28 rows and you have completed the last WS row.

Start to decrease to turn heel: continue in the same sl st pattern to reinforce heel. Starting with a RS row, knit until there are 9 sts left on LH needle. Decrease 1 st using ssk or skpo and turn work leaving 7 sts on the other needle. S1 purlwise and purl until 9 sts remain on LH needle. P2tog and turn work. S1 and continue in sl st pattern until there are 8 sts left on LH needle. Decrease using ssk or skpo and turn work. S1 purlwise and purl until 8 sts remain on LH needle. P2tog and turn work. Continue in the same way, reducing the number of sts at the sides on each row and keeping the same number of sts (12) in the middle.

When you run out of side sts, divide the heel flap sts between 2 needles (6–6). K6 to bring yarn to centre of heel, between needle 1 and needle 4.

FOOT

Pick up 16 sts from LH edge of heel flap using a spare needle. Knit the 6 sts from needle 1 and then the 16 picked up sts, turning sts knitwise. Work chart B pattern on needles 2 and 3 starting with chart round 1. Pick up and knit 16 sts from RH edge of heel flap turning sts knitwise. Using the same needle, knit the 6 sts on needle 4 (73 sts).

Start gusset decrease: k2tog at end of needle 1, and ssk or skpo at beginning of needle 4 on every second round. Continue following chart pattern on needles 2 and 3 and repeating chart rounds 1–20. Continue decreasing 2 gusset sts on every second round until there are 57 sts (14–15–14–14). Continue in st st on needles 1 and 4 and in chart pattern on needles 2 and 3. When you have knitted 49 rounds after the heel flap, and have completed chart round 9, start to decrease for the toe.

Work a wide wedge toe decrease on needles 1 and 4 and follow chart pattern on needles 2 and 3.
Needle 1: knit to last 3 sts, k2tog, k1.
Needle 4: k1, ssk, knit to end.
Work this decrease on every second round until there are 9 sts left on each needle. Then decrease on every round.
Needles 2 and 3: Work toe decreases following chart C (rounds 1–16).
Work until 8 sts remain. Break off yarn and thread through remaining sts.

Weave in ends and steam block lightly.

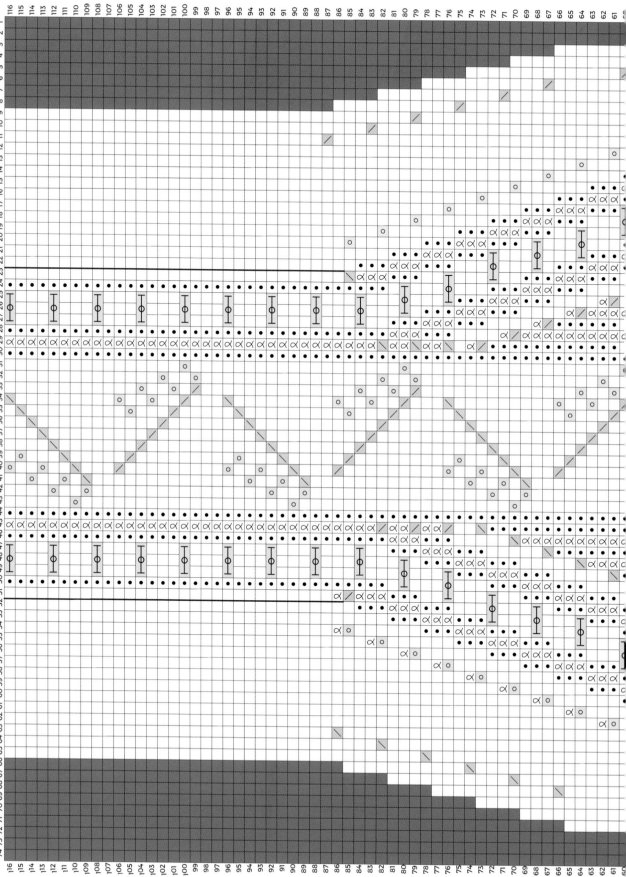

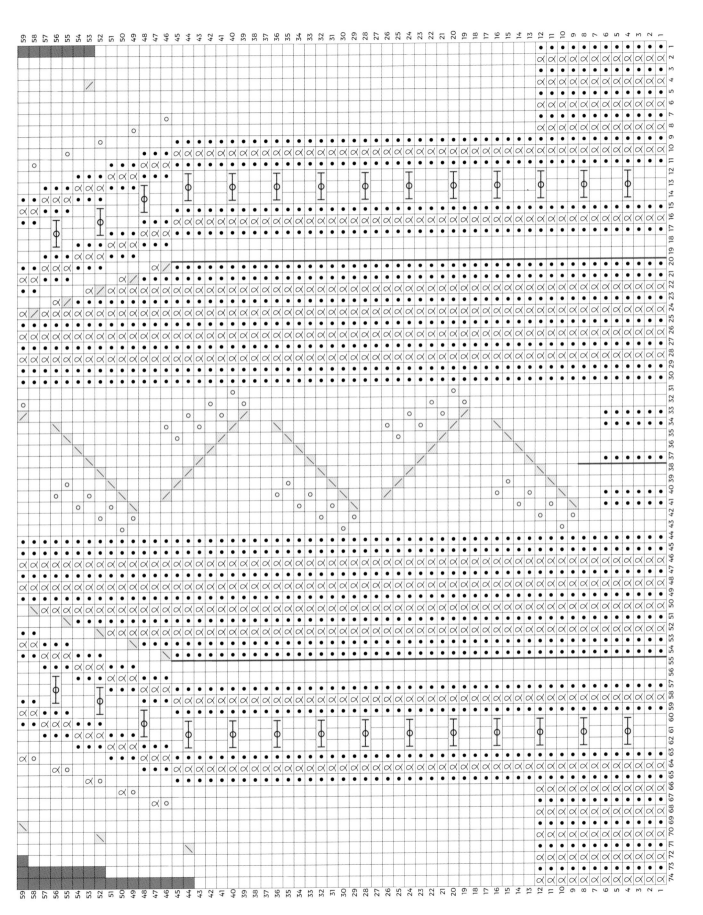

CHART B: FOOT

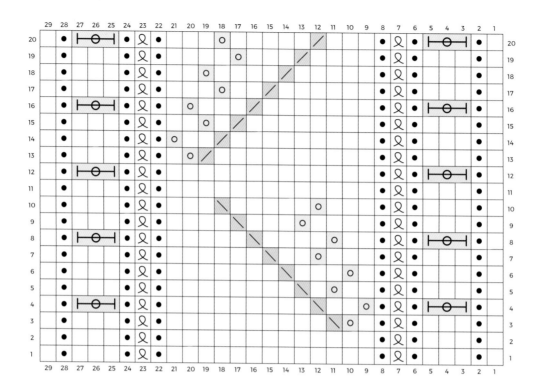

CHART C: TOE DECREASES

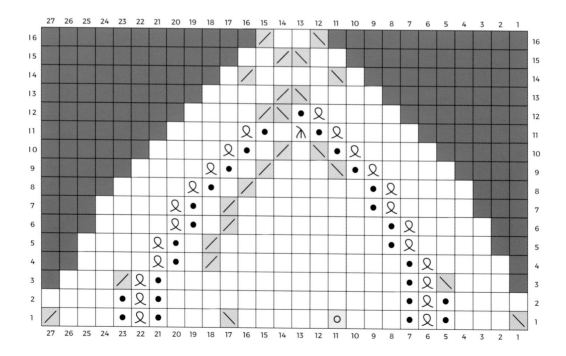

	knit		ssk: slip 2 sts knitwise one at a time onto RH needle, pass them back onto LH needle and knit them together through back loops
Q	knit through back loop	/	knit 2 together
●	purl	⋏	slip 1 st knitwise, knit 2 together and pass the slipped st over the knitted sts
	no st	o	yarn over
	next needle	o	yarn over from front
		⊢⊖⊣	slip 3 sts to RH needle, pass first slipped st over the other 2 slipped sts, move these 2 sts back to the LH needle and k1, yo, k1

Flirtation

*Dark eyes, brown hair. Flirting and storytelling,
red cheeks and a tender smile. These socks are
for people who are always relaxing company.
A beautiful cable design symbolizes fate causing
two people's paths to cross.*

SIZE: UK 5/6 (Europe 38/39, US 7½/8½)

YARN: 2 balls of Novita 7 Veljestä aran (10-ply/
worsted) yarn in Bark 694; 100g/200m/218yd

AMOUNT USED: 170g (6oz)

KNITTING NEEDLES: 3.5mm (UK 9/10, US 4)
DPN or size to obtain correct tension, cable needle

TENSION (GAUGE): 20 sts and 26 rows/
10cm (4in)

LEG

Cast on 68 sts and divide between 4 needles as
follows: 22–12–12–22. Join, being careful not to twist,
and work in the round. Work all 93 rounds of chart A.
Due to the decreases for the calf, there will be 50 sts
by the end.

Before starting the heel, divide them between the
needles as follows: 13–12–12–13. If you want a longer
leg, repeat chart rounds 86–93 once more.

HEEL

Start rib heel flap by knitting the sts on needle 1 onto needle 4 (26 sts). Leave remaining sts on needles 2 and 3. Turn work, s1 purlwise and purl to end of row. At the same time, decrease 2 sts (24 sts). Turn work.

Row 1 (RS): *s1, k1*, repeat from * to * to end of row. Turn work.
Row 2 (WS): s1 purlwise, p1, *k1, p1*, repeat from * to * to end of row.
Repeat these two rows until heel flap has 24 rows and you have completed the last WS row.

Start to decrease to turn heel: continue in the same rib pattern to reinforce heel. Starting with a RS row, knit until there are 9 sts left on the LH needle. Decrease 1 st using skpo and turn work leaving 7 sts on the other needle. S1 purlwise and purl until 9 sts remain on LH needle. P2tog and turn work. S1 and continue in rib pattern until 8 sts remain on LH needle. Decrease using skpo and turn work. S1 purlwise and purl until 8 sts remain on LH needle. P2tog and turn work. Continue in the same way, reducing the number of sts at the sides on each row and keeping the same number of sts (8) in the middle.

When you run out of side sts, divide the heel flap sts between 2 needles (4–4). K4 to bring yarn to centre of heel, between needle 1 and needle 4.

FOOT

Pick up 14 sts from LH edge of heel flap using a spare needle. Knit the 4 sts from needle 1 and then the 14 picked up sts, turning sts knitwise. Work chart B pattern on needles 2 and 3 starting with chart round 1. Pick up and knit 14 sts from RH edge of heel flap turning sts knitwise. Using the same needle, knit the 4 sts on needle 4 (60 sts).

Start gusset decrease: k2tog at end of needle 1, and ssk or skpo at beginning of needle 4 on every second round. Continue following chart pattern on needles 2 and 3 and repeating chart rounds 1–8. Continue decreasing 2 gusset sts on every second round until there are 48 sts (12–12–12–12).

Continue in st st on needles 1 and 4 and in chart pattern on needles 2 and 3. When you have knitted 44 rounds after the heel flap, and have completed chart round 4, start to decrease for the toe.

Work a wide wedge toe decrease on needles 1 and 4 and follow chart pattern on needles 2 and 3:
Needle 1: knit to last 3 sts, k2tog, k1.
Needle 4: k1, ssk, knit to end.
Work this decrease on every second round until there are 7 sts left on each needle. Then decrease on every round.
Needles 2 and 3: work toe decreases following chart C (rounds 1–14).
Work until 8 sts remain. Break off yarn and thread through remaining sts.

Weave in ends and steam block lightly.

CHART A: LEG

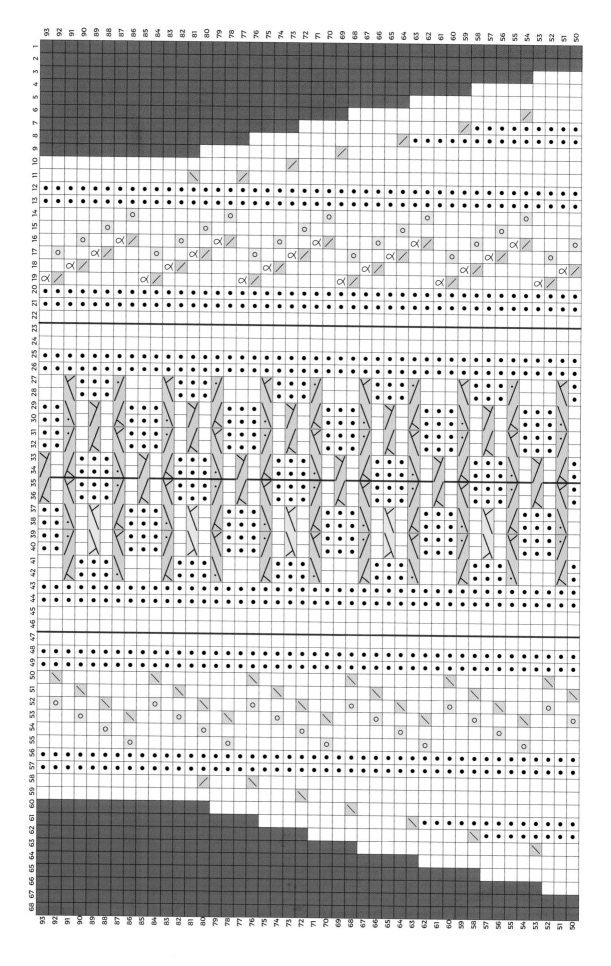

CHART B: FOOT

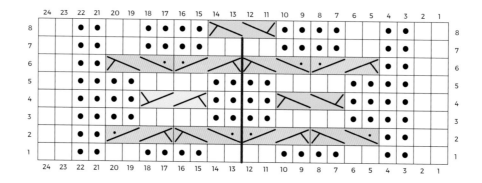

CHART C: TOE DECREASES

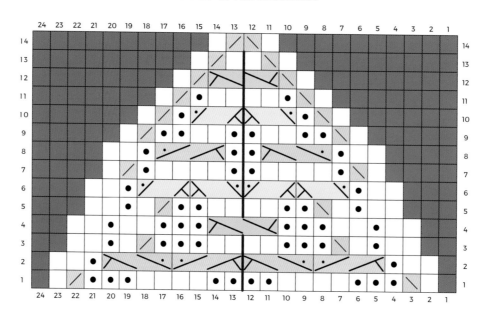

☐	knit	
☒	knit through back loop	
●	purl	
╱	knit 2 together	
○	yarn over	
▨	no st	
☐	next needle	

ssk: slip 2 sts knitwise one at a time onto RH needle, pass them back onto LH needle and knit them together through back loops

place 2 sts on cable needle and bring to front of work, k2 and k2 from cable needle

place 2 sts on cable needle and bring to back of work, k2 and k2 from cable needle

place 2 sts on cable needle and bring to front of work, p2 and k2 from cable needle

place 2 sts on cable needle and bring to back of work, k2 and p2 from cable needle

place 2 sts on cable needle and bring to front of work, p1 and k2 from cable needle

place 1 st on cable needle and bring to back of work, k2 and p1 from cable needle

Adventure

The rustling of leaves, the colours of autumn, and laughter on a crisp autumn day. These socks are an adventure in different colour combinations. Sit peacefully under a blanket and let the threads run through your fingers, creating a tale of your own.

SIZE: UK 6 (Europe 39, US 8½)

YARN: 3 balls of Gjestal Janne aran (10-ply/worsted) yarn in Wine Red 421 (A) and 2 balls in Orange 436 (B); 50g/100m/109yd

AMOUNT USED: 130–140g (4½–5oz) A, 75–80g (2½–2¾oz) B

KNITTING NEEDLES: 3.5mm (UK 9/10, US 4) DPN or size to obtain correct tension

TENSION (GAUGE): 20 sts and 26 rows/10cm (4in)

BEFORE YOU START
The chart is read from bottom to top and from right to left. The instructions include two different sizes (medium and wide). The width of the leg on chart A1 will fit a calf measuring about 35–39cm (13¾–15¼in) and the width of the leg on chart A2 will fit a calf measuring about 40–45cm (15¾–17¾in). The heel and foot are knitted following the same instructions for both sizes.

LEG (MEDIUM)

Cast on 65 sts in yarn A and divide sts between 4 needles as follows: 16–17–16–16. Join, being careful not to twist, and work in the round.

Work rib following rounds 1–8 of chart A1. Work chart round 9 in st st.

Start the Fair Isle pattern at round 10 of chart A1 and work leg following chart, decreasing in a suitable place at beginning of needle 1 and end of needle 4 on the following rounds:

Decreases:
Round 48: decrease 2 sts (63 sts).
Round 60: decrease 2 sts (61 sts).
Note: on round 66, divide sts between needles as follows: 18–13–12–18.
Round 67: decrease 2 sts (59 sts).
Round 73: decrease 2 sts (57 sts).
Round 78: decrease 2 sts (55 sts).
Round 83: decrease 2 sts (53 sts).
Round 88: decrease 2 sts (51 sts).

When you have worked all 102 rounds for the leg, check that sts are divided between needles as follows: 13–13–12–13.

LEG (WIDE)

Cast on 70 sts in yarn A and divide sts between 4 needles as follows: 17–19–18–16. Join, being careful not to twist, and work in the round. Work rib following rounds 1–8 of chart A2. Work chart round 9 in st st, increasing 3 sts at the same time. Check that sts are divided between needles as follows: 18–19–18–18.

Start the Fair Isle pattern at round 10 of chart A2 and work leg following chart, decreasing in a suitable place at beginning of needle 1 and end of needle 4 on the following rounds:

Decreases:
Round 34: decrease 2 sts (71 sts).
Round 48: decrease 2 sts (69 sts).
Round 54: decrease 2 sts (67 sts).
Round 60: decrease 2 sts (65 sts).

Note: on round 66, divide sts between needles as follows: 20–13–12–20.
Round 67: decrease 2 sts (63 sts).
Round 72: decrease 2 sts (61 sts).
Round 76: decrease 2 sts (59 sts).
Round 80: decrease 2 sts (57 sts).
Round 84: decrease 2 sts (55 sts).
Round 88: decrease 2 sts (53 sts).
Round 91: decrease 2 sts (51 sts).

When you have worked all 102 rounds for the leg, check that sts are divided between needles as follows: 13–13–12–13.

HEEL

Start reinforced heel flap in yarn A by knitting the sts on needle 1 onto needle 4 (26 sts for heel flap). Leave remaining sts on needles 2 and 3. Turn work, s1 purlwise and purl to end of row. At the same time, decrease 2 sts making 24 sts for heel flap. Turn work.

Row 1 (RS): *s1, k1*, repeat from * to * to end of row. Turn work.
Row 2 (WS): s1 purlwise and purl to end of row. Turn work.
Repeat these two rows until the reinforced heel flap has 24 rows and you have completed the last WS row.

Start to decrease to turn heel: continue in the same sl st pattern to reinforce heel. Starting with a RS row, knit until there are 9 sts left on the LH needle. Decrease 1 st using skpo and turn work leaving 7 sts on the other needle. S1 purlwise and purl until 9 sts remain on LH needle. P2tog and turn work. S1 knitwise and continue in sl st pattern until 8 sts remain on LH needle. Decrease using skpo and turn work. S1 purlwise and purl until 8 sts remain on LH needle. P2tog and turn work. Continue in the same way, reducing the number of sts at the sides on each row and keeping the same number of sts (8) in the middle.

When you run out of side sts, divide the heel flap sts between 2 needles (4–4). Knit sts on needle 4 to bring yarn between needles 4 and 1.

FOOT

Pick up 14 sts from side of heel flap with needle 1 and pick up 14 sts from other side of heel flap with needle 4 (61 sts). Continue Fair Isle pattern starting at round 1 of chart B. Knit the sts picked up from the edge of the heel flap, turning sts knitwise.

Start gusset decrease: k2tog at end of needle 1 and ssk or skpo at beginning of needle 4 on rounds as shown in chart B (rounds 2, 4, 6, 8, 10 and 12). The grey squares on the chart represent places where there are no sts. After the gusset decrease there will be 49 sts (12–13–12–12). Continue the Fair Isle pattern following the chart.

When you have worked 37 rounds of chart B, work one more round in yarn A and decrease 1 st at end of needle 4. Divide so that there are 12 sts on each needle.

Finish sock with a wide wedge toe in yarn A:
Needles 1 and 3: knit to last 3 sts, k2tog, k1.
Needles 2 and 4: k1, ssk or skpo, knit to end.
Work the decreases on every second round. Once there are 8 sts left on each needle (32 in total), work decreases on every round. When there are 8 sts left, break off yarn and thread through remaining sts.

Weave in ends and steam block lightly.

■	knit (in yarn A)
▧	knit (in yarn B)
⊙	purl (in yarn A)
╱	knit 2 together (in yarn A)
╲	ssk: slip 2 sts knitwise one at a time onto RH needle, pass them back onto LH needle and knit them together through back loops (in yarn A)
╱	ssk: slip 2 sts knitwise one at a time onto right-
╲	knit 2 together (in yarn B)
▦	no st
☐	next needle

CHART A1: MEDIUM LEG

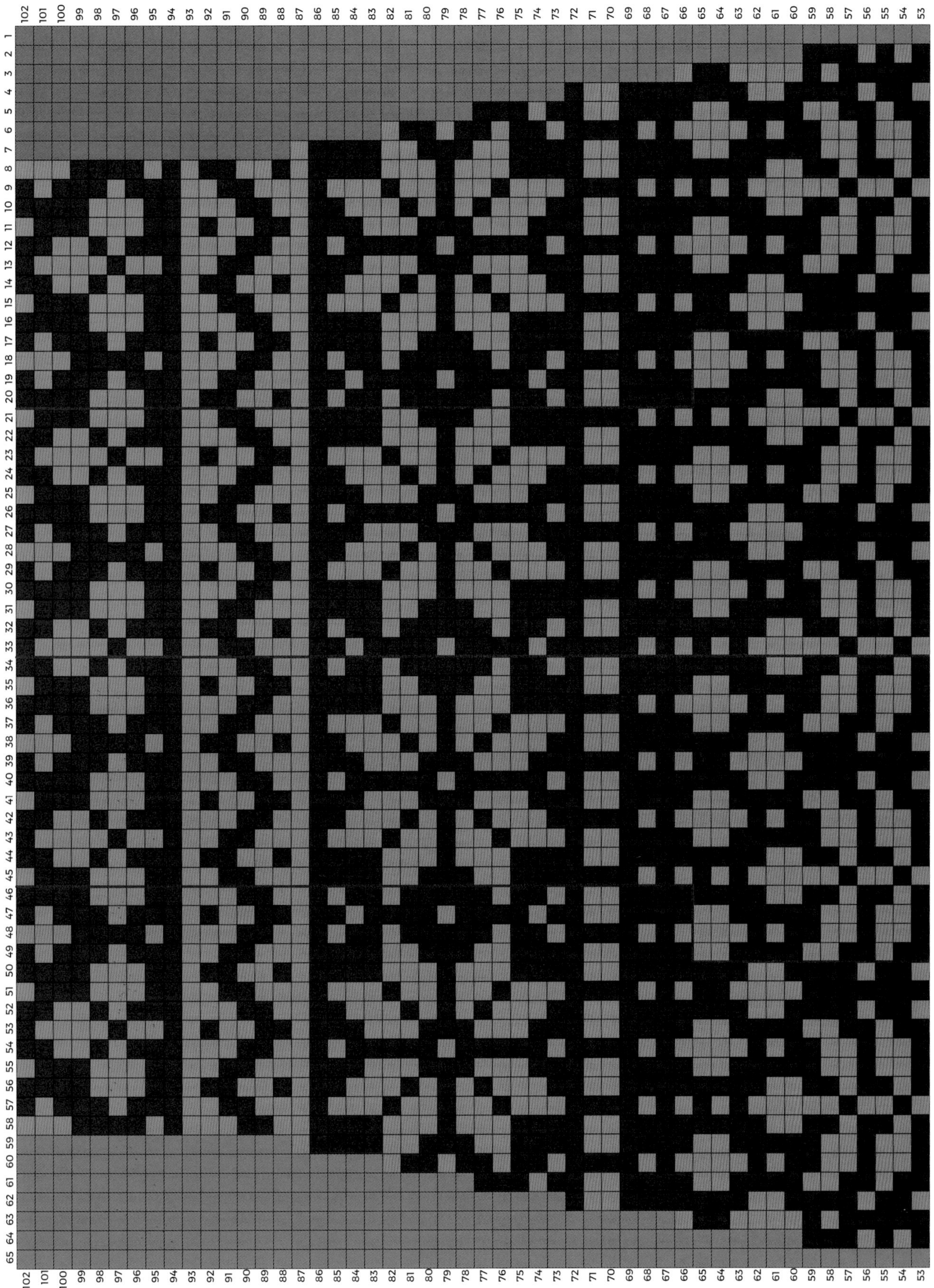

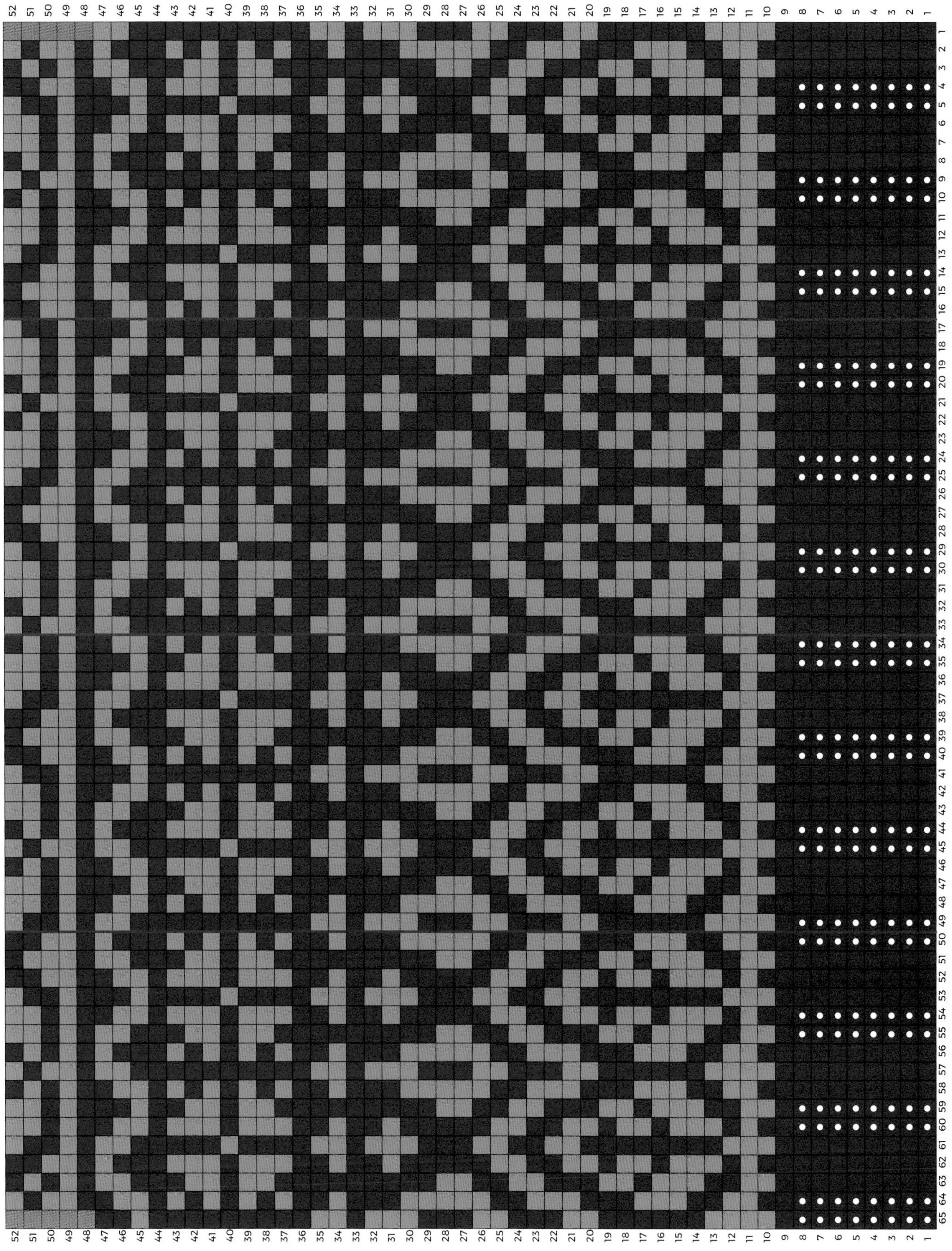

CHART A2: WIDE LEG

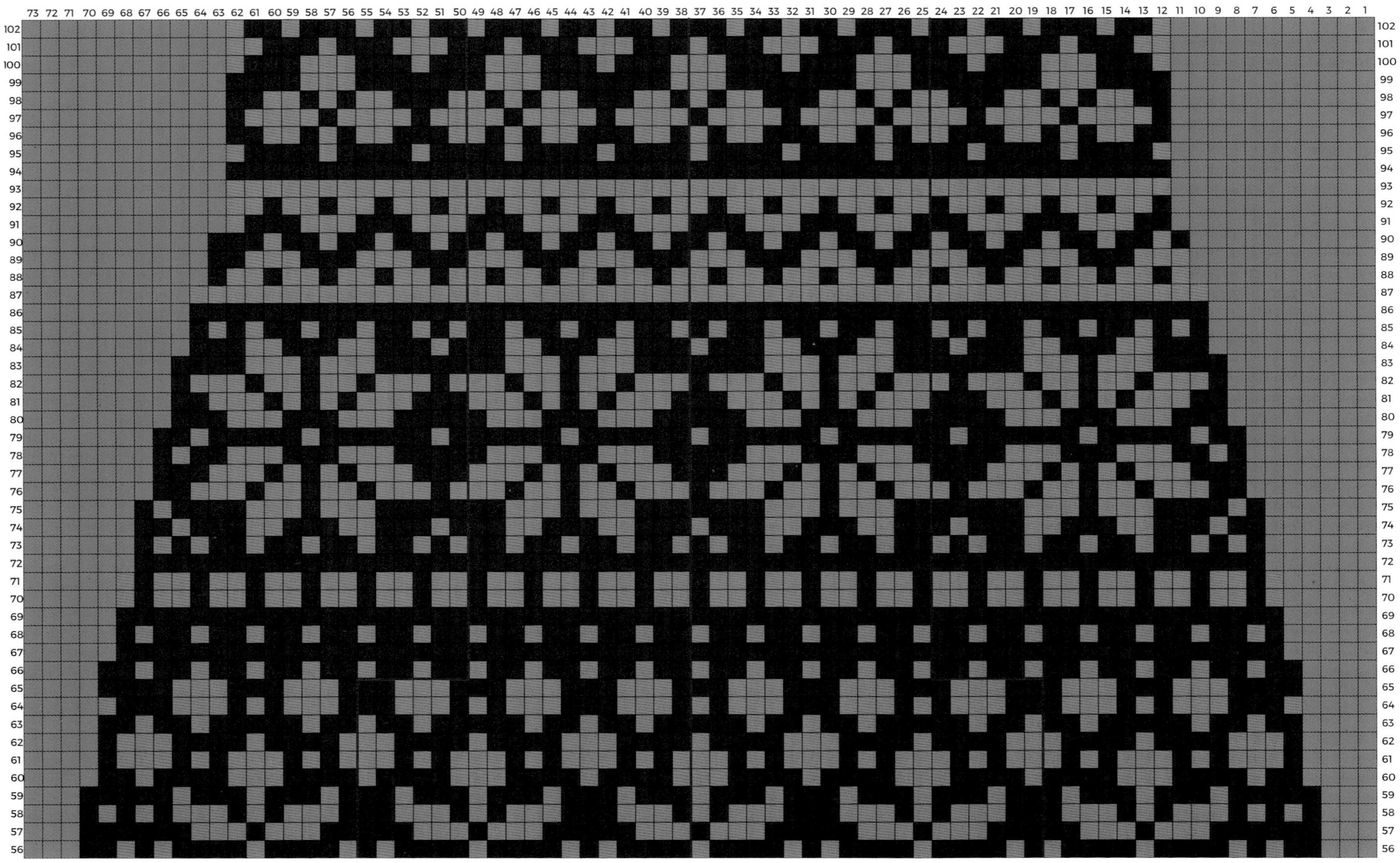

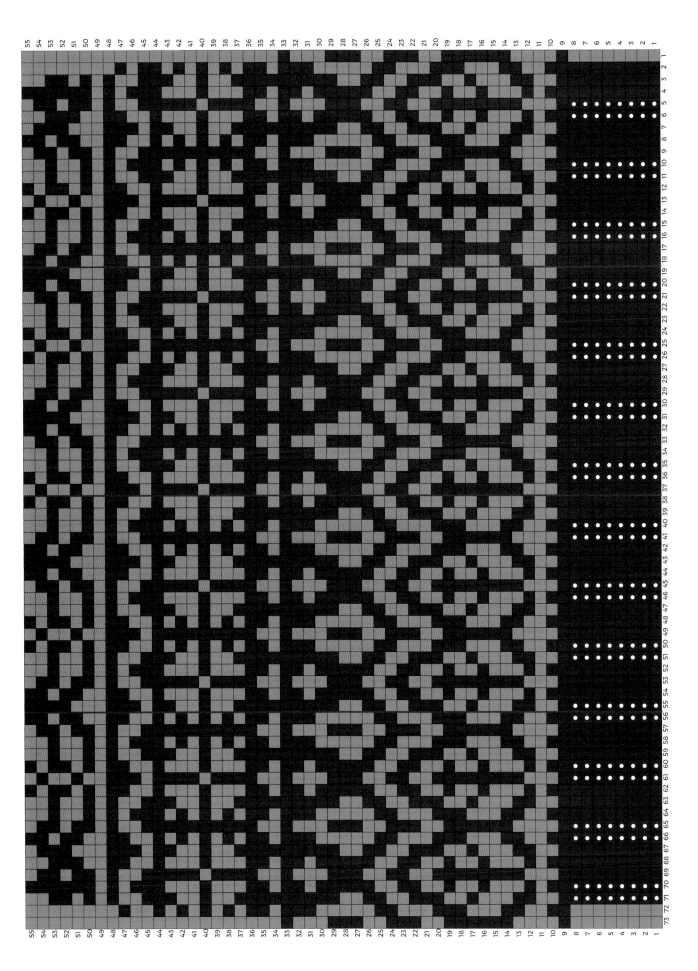

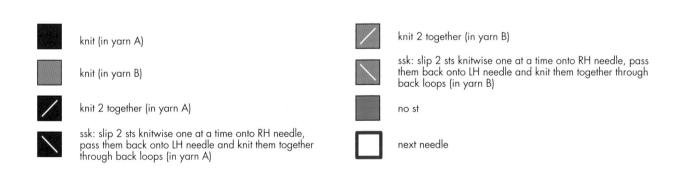

knit (in yarn A)

knit (in yarn B)

knit 2 together (in yarn A)

ssk: slip 2 sts knitwise one at a time onto RH needle, pass them back onto LH needle and knit them together through back loops (in yarn A)

knit 2 together (in yarn B)

ssk: slip 2 sts knitwise one at a time onto RH needle, pass them back onto LH needle and knit them together through back loops (in yarn B)

no st

next needle

Soulmates

With these beautiful soulmates it is time to pause, say farewell to the last vestiges of summer, and float ahead on the autumn breeze towards new challenges.

SIZE: UK 5/6 (Europe 38/39, US 7½/8½)

YARN: 1 ball of Schachenmayr Premium Silk 4-ply (fingering) in Linen 05; 100g/400m/437yd

AMOUNT USED: 63g (2¼oz)

KNITTING NEEDLES: 2.5mm (UK 12/13, US 1/2) DPN or size to obtain correct tension, cable needle

TENSION (GAUGE): 28 sts and 36 rows/ 10cm (4in)

BEFORE YOU START
In the charts for the leg, needles 1 and 2 form the back of the sock and needles 3 and 4 form the front of the sock. After the heel, the needle numbering changes and needles 1 and 4 are used for the sole of the sock and needles 2 and 3 for the top.

Instead of the cable heel, you could work an ordinary reinforced heel in slip st. See *Foolish Love* on page 70 for instructions.

LEG

Cast on 63 sts and divide between 4 needles as follows: 20–16–13–14. Join, being careful not to twist, and work in the round.

Work leg following chart A (60 rounds). After the last round of the chart, change the number of sts on each needle by knitting the first 5 sts on needle 1 to needle 4. This gives you 31 sts for the heel flap (shown in the pale green squares on the chart). Move these heel sts onto one needle and leave the sts on needles 3 and 4 (32 sts).

HEEL

Work the heel following chart B. Always slip the first st knitwise on RS and purlwise on WS. Work all 30 rounds of chart B.

Start to decrease to turn heel and work in st st: starting with a RS row, knit until there are 11 sts left on LH needle. Decrease 1 st using ssk or skpo and turn work leaving 9 sts on the other needle. S1 purlwise and purl until 11 sts remain on LH needle. P2tog and turn work. Slip 1 and continue in st st until there are 10 sts left on LH needle. Decrease using ssk or skpo and turn work. S1 purlwise and purl until 10 sts remain on LH needle. P2tog and turn work. Continue in the same way, reducing the number of sts at the sides on each row and keeping the same number of sts (11) in the middle.

When you run out of side sts, divide the heel flap sts between 2 needles (6–5). K4 then k2tog to bring yarn to centre of heel, between needle 1 and needle 4.

FOOT

Pick up 16 sts from LH edge of heel flap using a spare needle. Knit the 5 sts from needle 1 and then the 16 picked up sts, turning sts knitwise. Work chart C pattern on needles 2 and 3 starting with chart round 7. Pick up and knit 16 sts from RH edge of heel flap turning sts knitwise. Using the same needle, knit the 5 sts on needle 4 (74 sts).

Start gusset decrease: k2tog at end of needle 1, and ssk or skpo at beginning of needle 4 on every second round. Continue following chart C on needles 2 and 3 and repeating chart rounds 1–12. Continue decreasing 2 gusset sts on every second round until there are 64 sts (16–16–16–16).

Continue in st st on needles 1 and 4 and in chart pattern on needles 2 and 3. When you have worked 55 rounds counted from the edge of the heel flap and have completed chart round 1, start to decrease for the toe.

Work toe decreases following chart D. Work until 9 sts remain. Break off yarn and thread through remaining sts.

Weave in ends and steam lightly to block.

knit

•   purl

Ϙ   knit through back loop

~   purl through back loop

/   knit 2 together

o   yarn over

\   ssk: slip 2 sts knitwise one at a time onto RH needle, pass them back onto LH needle and knit them together through back loops

⋀   slip 2 sts knitwise as if you were knitting them together, knit 1 st and pass the slipped sts over the knitted st

place 1 st on cable needle and bring to front of work, k1 and k1 from cable needle

place 1 st on cable needle and bring to back of work, k1 and k1 from cable needle

place 1 st on cable needle and bring to front of work, p1 and k1 from cable needle

place 1 st on cable needle and bring to back of work, k1 and p1 from cable needle

⋏   slip 1 st knitwise, knit 2 together and pass the slipped st over the knitted sts

next needle

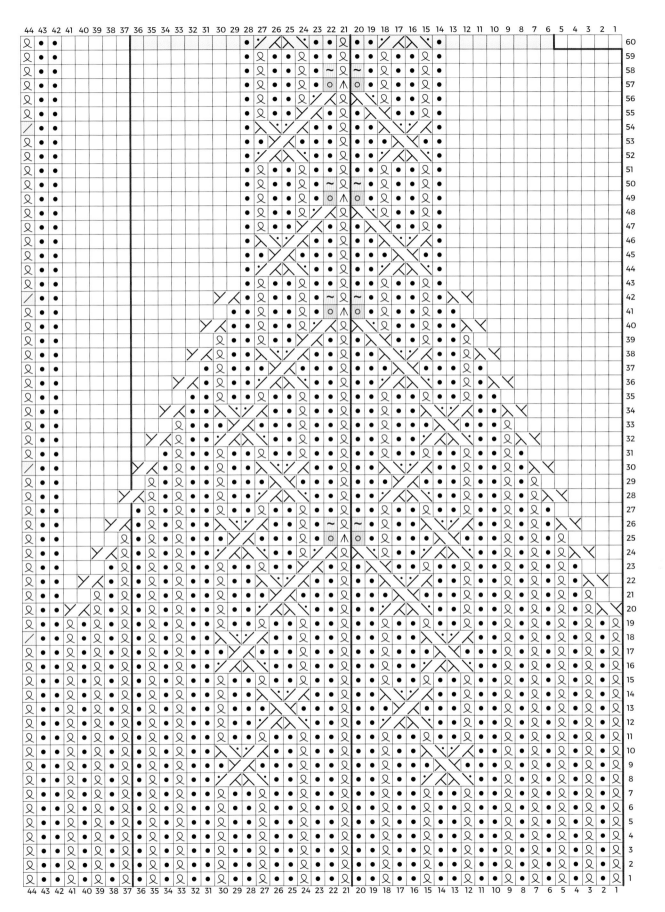

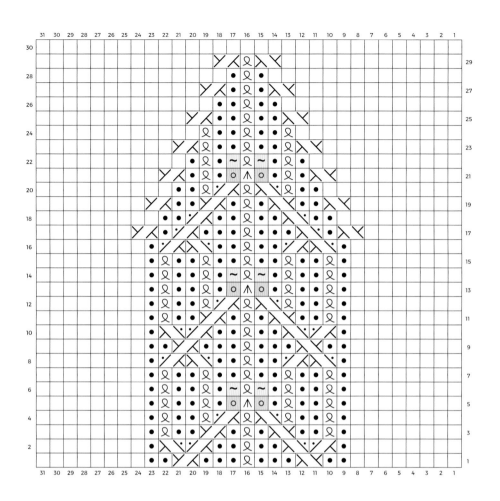

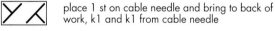

	knit on RS, purl on WS			place 1 st onto a cable needle and bring to front of work, k1 and k1 from cable needle
Ω	knit through back loop on RS, purl through back loop on WS			place 1 st on cable needle and bring to back of work, k1 and k1 from cable needle
●	purl on RS, knit on WS			place 1 st on cable needle and bring to front of work, p1 and k1 from cable needle (RS and WS)
O	yarn over			place 1 st on cable needle and bring to back of work, k1 and p1 from cable needle (RS and WS)
∧	slip 2 sts knitwise as if you were knitting them together, knit 1 st and pass the slipped sts over the knitted st			
~	purl through back loop on RS, knit through back loop on WS			

CHART C: FOOT

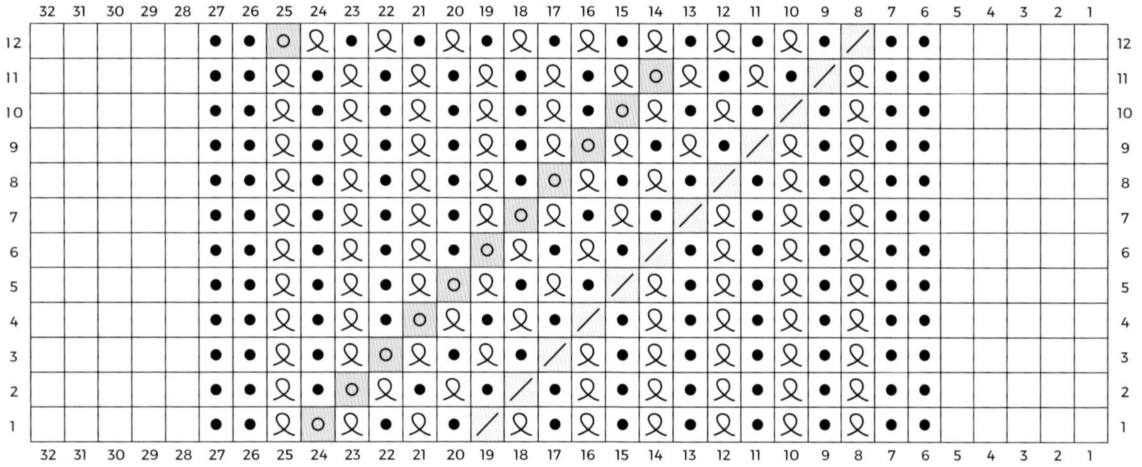

A knitting chart with columns numbered 32 down to 1 (left to right) and rows numbered 1 to 12 (bottom to top). The chart uses the following symbols.

Legend:

(blank)	knit
●	purl
Ω	knit through back loop
/	knit 2 together
o	yarn over
□	next needle

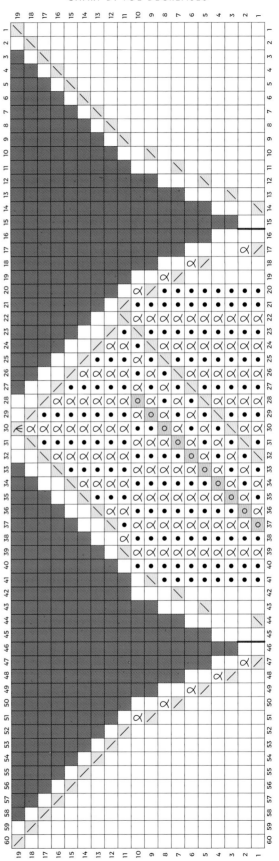

knit

● purl

Ω knit through back loop

／ knit 2 together

○ yarn over

＼ ssk: slip 2 sts knitwise one at a time onto RH needle, pass them back onto LH needle and knit them together through back loops

⋏ slip 1 st knitwise, knit 2 together and pass the slipped st over the knitted sts

no st

next needle

Lake Tiilikka

*On the shore of Lake Tiilikka in the north of Finland, looking
out through the flaps of the tent at dawn, the first snow softly
falls to the ground. An enchanting lake landscape, fresh air
and clean, pristine snow make the coming winter feel magical.*

SIZE: UK 5/6 (Europe 38/39, US 7½/8½); calf
circumference: 33–38cm (13–15in)

YARN: 1 ball of Novita Nalle DK (8-ply/light
worsted) in Jeans 160 (A) and 1 ball in Linen 061
(B); 100g/260m/284yd

AMOUNT USED: 80g (2¾oz) A, 80g (2¾oz) B

KNITTING NEEDLES: 3mm (UK 11, US 2/3)
DPN or size to obtain correct tension, cable needle

TENSION (GAUGE): 24 sts and 32 rows/
10cm (4in)

BEFORE YOU START

If desired, you can use needles half a millimetre
smaller or equivalent for the rib section to prevent the
cuff from sagging.

If you want to make these socks for a larger calf
size, change to 3.5mm (UK 9/10, US 4) needles for
the Fair Isle pattern. This will produce socks for a calf
circumference of more than 40cm (15¾in).

If you want a larger foot size, knit round 40 more
times before starting to decrease for the toe.

LEG

Cast on 72 sts in yarn A and divide between 4 needles with 18 sts on each. Join, being careful not to twist, and work in the round.

Start in rib following chart A and knit 13 rounds in rib. After the rib, start the Fair Isle pattern at chart round 14. Work leg following chart, decreasing in a suitable place at beginning of needle 1 and end of needle 4 on the following rounds:

Decrease on rounds: 41, 49, 55, 60, 64 and 68 (60 sts). *Note: on round 58 change the number of sts on each needle to 18–15–15–18.*

When you have worked all 80 rounds for the leg, divide sts so there are 15 on each needle.

HEEL

Start twisted reinforced heel flap by knitting the sts on needle 1 onto needle 4 (30 sts for heel flap). Leave remaining sts on needles 2 and 3. Turn work, s1 purlwise and purl to end of row. Turn work.

Row 1 (RS): s1, k1, *s1 purlwise with yarn in front, k1*, repeat from * to * to end of row. Turn work.
Row 2 (WS): s1 purlwise and purl to end of row. Turn work.
Repeat these two rows until heel flap has 30 rows and you have completed the last WS row.

Start to decrease to turn heel: continue in the same sl st pattern to reinforce heel. Starting with a RS row, knit until there are 11 sts left on LH needle. Decrease 1 st using ssk or skpo and turn work, leaving 9 sts on the other needle. S1 purlwise and purl until 11 sts remain on LH needle. P2tog and turn work. Slip 1 knitwise and continue in sl st pattern until there are 10 sts left on LH needle. Decrease using ssk or skpo and turn work. S1 purlwise and purl until 10 sts remain on LH needle. P2tog and turn work. Continue in the same way, reducing the number of sts at the sides on each row and keeping the same number of sts (10) in the middle.

When you run out of side sts, divide the heel flap sts between 2 needles (5–5). K5 to bring yarn to centre of heel, between needle 1 and needle 4.

FOOT

Pick up 17 sts from side of heel flap with needle 1 and pick up 17 sts from other side of heel flap with needle 4 (74 sts). Start Fair Isle pattern starting from round 1 of chart B. At the same time, increase 1 st on needle 3. Knit the sts picked up from the edge of the heel flap, turning sts knitwise.

Start gusset decrease: k2tog at end of needle 1, and ssk or skpo at beginning of needle 4 on rounds as shown in chart B (rounds 2, 4, 6, 8, 10, 12 and 14). The grey squares on the chart represent places where there are no sts. After the gusset decrease there will be 61 sts (15–16–15–15).

Continue in Fair Isle pattern until you have completed all 41 rounds of chart B. On last round of chart decrease 1 st and divide sts so there are 15 sts on each needle.

Finish sock in yarn B, working a wide wedge toe:
Needles 1 and 3: knit to last 3 sts, k2tog, k1.
Needles 2 and 4: k1; ssk or skpo, knit to end.
Work the decreases on every second round. Once there are 10 sts left on each needle, work decreases on every round. When there are 8 sts left, break off yarn and thread through remaining sts.

Weave in ends and steam block lightly.

CHART A: LEG

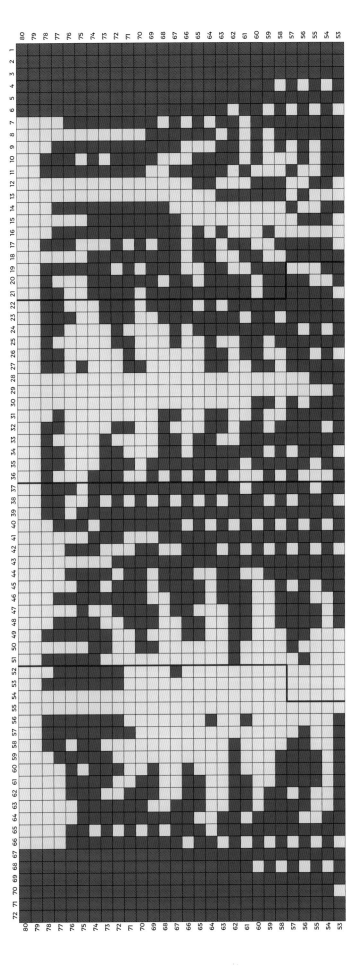

knit (in yarn A)

knit (in yarn B)

purl (in yarn A)

place 1 st on cable needle and bring to front of work, k1 and k1 from cable needle (in yarn A)

place 1 st on cable needle and bring to back of work, k1 and k1 from cable needle (in yarn A)

no st

next needle

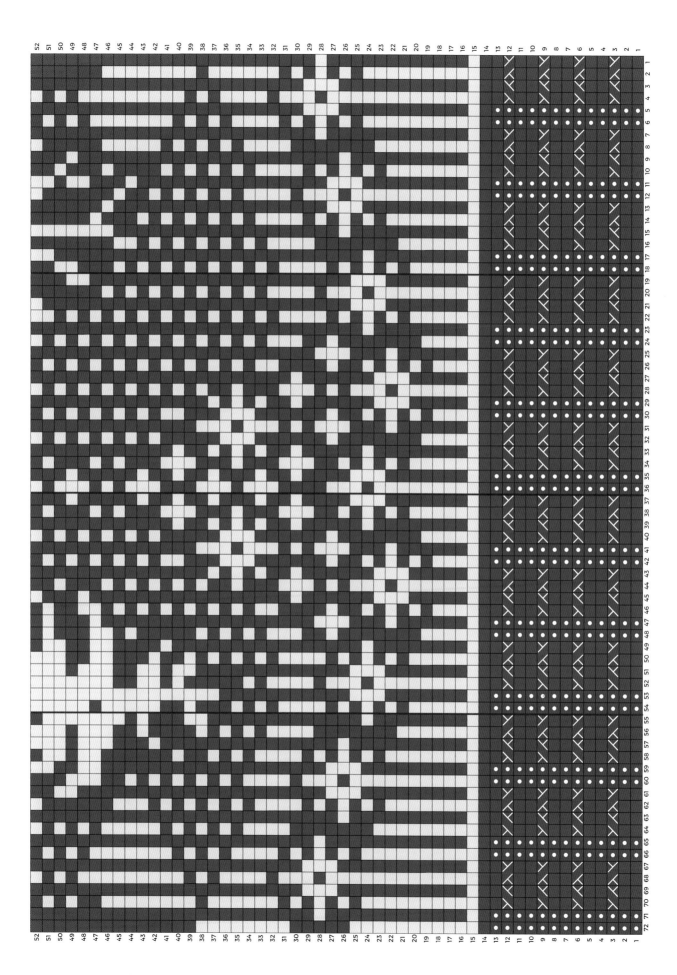

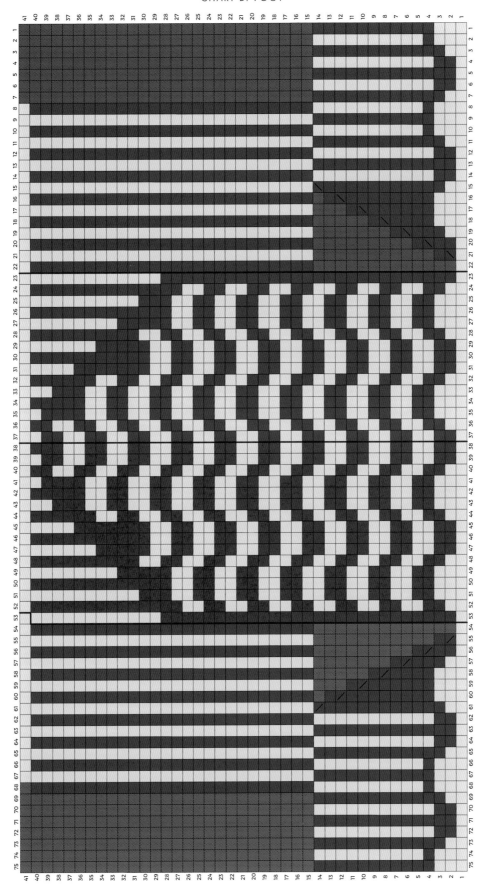

knit (in yarn A)

knit (in yarn B)

purl (in yarn A)

knit 2 together (in yarn A)

ssk: slip 2 sts knitwise one at a time onto RH needle, pass them back onto LH needle and knit them together through back loops (in yarn A)

no st

next needle

WINTER

winter

Frozen Seas

Slightly glacial, cool and icy but still lovely, Frozen Seas *invoke the feeling of winter. A cable design runs down the back of these lace socks, continuing all the way to the heel. This design is a joy to knit and the socks simply appear like the first morning frost.*

SIZE: UK 4 (Europe 37, US 6½) and UK 6 (Europe 39, US 8½)

YARN: 2 balls of Lana Grossa Meilenweit 4-ply (fingering) yarn in Mint-turquoise 1376; 50g/210m/230yd

AMOUNT USED: 60g (2oz)–65g (2¼oz)

KNITTING NEEDLES: 2.5mm (UK 12/13, US 1/2) DPN or size to obtain correct tension

TENSION (GAUGE): 28 sts and 36 rows/10cm (4in)

BEFORE YOU START
You can knit either size from the same written instructions. The instructions are identical until the end of the gusset decrease. After that, the differences for the larger size are shown in blue.

In the charts for the leg, needles 1 and 2 form the back of the sock and needles 3 and 4 form the front of the sock. After the heel, the needle numbering changes and needles 1 and 4 are used for the sole of the sock and needles 2 and 3 for the top.

LEG

Cast on 63 sts and divide between 4 needles as follows: 16–16–16–15. Join, being careful not to twist, and work in the round.

First work rib following rounds 1–6 of chart A, then work round 7 of chart increasing 1 st on needle 4 at the same time. Then continue leg following chart A, repeating chart rounds 8–17.

Once you have worked 57 rounds of the leg, including the rib, and completed chart round 17, start to work the heel on needles 1 and 2 (32 sts for heel flap). Leave the other sts on needles 3 and 4.

HEEL

Work heel following chart B and repeating rows 1–10 until the heel flap has 30 rows and you have completed chart row 10. Always slip the first st knitwise on RS and purlwise on WS.

Start to decrease to turn heel and work in st st: starting with a RS row, knit until there are 11 sts left on LH needle. Decrease 1 st using ssk or skpo and turn work leaving 9 sts on the other needle. S1 purlwise and purl until 11 sts remain on LH needle. P2tog and turn work. Slip 1 and continue in st st until there are 10 sts left on LH needle. Decrease using ssk or skpo and turn work. S1 purlwise and purl until 10 sts remain on LH needle. P2tog and turn work. Continue in the same way, reducing the number of sts at the sides on each row and keeping the same number of sts (12) in the middle.

When you run out of side sts, divide the heel flap sts between 2 needles (6–6). K6 to bring yarn to centre of heel, between needle 1 and needle 4.

FOOT

Pick up 16 sts from LH edge of heel flap using a spare needle. Knit the 6 sts from needle 1 and then the 16 picked up sts, turning sts knitwise. Work chart C pattern on needles 2 and 3 starting with chart round 1. Pick up and knit 16 sts from RH edge of heel flap turning sts knitwise. Using the same needle, knit the 6 sts on needle 4 (76 sts).

Start gusset decrease: k2tog at end of needle 1, and ssk or skpo at beginning of needle 4 on every second round. Continue following chart pattern on needles 2 and 3 and repeating chart rounds 1–10. Continue decreasing 2 gusset sts on every second round until there are 60 sts (14–16–16–14) – 64 sts (16–16–16–16).

Continue in st st on needles 1 and 4 and in chart pattern on needles 2 and 3. When you have worked 55 (60) rounds counted from the edge of the heel flap and have worked to the end of chart row 5 (10), work one more round and for the smaller size divide sts so there are 15 sts on each needle.

Finish sock with a wide wedge toe:
Needles 1 and 3: knit to last 3 sts, k2tog, k1.
Needles 2 and 4: k1, ssk or skpo; knit to end.
First work the decreases on every second round. Once there are 32 sts left (8–8–8–8), work the decreases on every round. When there are 8 sts left, break off yarn and thread through remaining sts.

Weave in ends and steam block lightly.

CHART A: LEG

KEY TO CHARTS A AND C

knit

knit through back loop

purl

knit 2 together

ssk: slip 2 sts knitwise one at a time onto RH needle, pass them back onto LH needle and knit them together through back loops

yarn over

place 2 sts on cable needle and bring to front of work, k2 and k2 from cable needle

place 2 sts on cable needle and bring to back of work, k2 and k2 from cable needle

no st

next needle

CHART B: HEEL

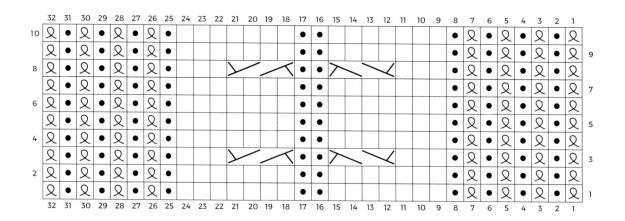

KEY TO CHART B

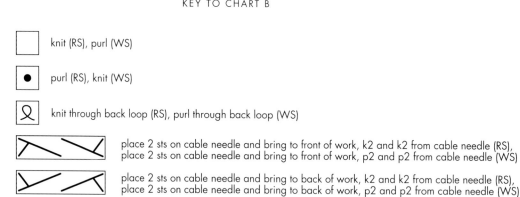

☐ knit (RS), purl (WS)

● purl (RS), knit (WS)

Ⴍ knit through back loop (RS), purl through back loop (WS)

⟋⟍ place 2 sts on cable needle and bring to front of work, k2 and k2 from cable needle (RS), place 2 sts on cable needle and bring to front of work, p2 and p2 from cable needle (WS)

⟍⟋ place 2 sts on cable needle and bring to back of work, k2 and k2 from cable needle (RS), place 2 sts on cable needle and bring to back of work, p2 and p2 from cable needle (WS)

CHART C: FOOT

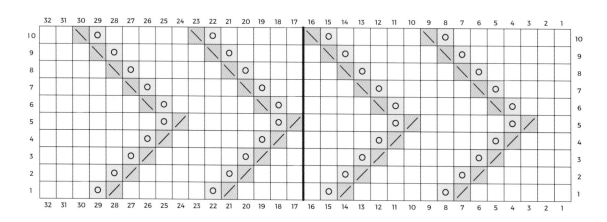

Longing

Still slightly pining for summer and remembering the bright moments of autumn, these knitted pathways lead you to crisp, frosty days and winter landscapes. Warming socks to wear while cradling a cup of coffee as the sun rises; a moment of peace before once more stepping into a new day of adventure.

SIZE: UK 6 (Europe 39, US 8½)

YARN: 2 balls of Novita 7 Veljestä aran (10-ply/worsted) yarn in Stone 043; 100g/200m/218yd

AMOUNT USED: 115g (4oz)

KNITTING NEEDLES: 3.5mm (UK 9/10, US 4) DPN or size to obtain correct tension, cable needle

TENSION (GAUGE): 21 sts and 26 rows/10cm (4in)

BEFORE YOU START
The right and left socks are mirror images of each other. Use charts A1, B1 and C1 for the right sock and charts A2, B2 and C2 for the left sock.

When to switch to the next needle is marked on the chart. This does change as the work progresses due to increases and decreases. Just make sure there are the same number of sts on each needle before starting the heel.

LEG

Right:

Cast on 50 sts and divide between 4 needles as follows: 13–11–12–14. Join, being careful not to twist, and work in the round. Work all 46 rounds of chart A1.

Left:

Cast on 50 sts and divide between 4 needles as follows: 14–12–11–13. Join, being careful not to twist, and work in the round. Work all 46 rounds of chart A2.

HEEL (RIGHT AND LEFT)

Start the decorative reinforced heel flap by knitting the sts on needle 1 onto needle 4 (27 sts for heel flap). Leave remaining sts on needles 2 and 3. Turn work, s1 purlwise and purl to end of row. At the same time, decrease 3 sts making 24 sts for heel flap. Turn work.

Row 1 (RS): *s1, k1*, repeat from * to * to end of row. Turn work.

Row 2 (WS): s1 purlwise and purl to end of row. Turn work.

Row 3 (RS): s1, k1, *k1, s1*, repeat from * to * until 2 sts remain, k2 and turn work.

Row 4 (WS): s1 purlwise and purl to end of row. Turn work.

Repeat these four rows until the heel flap has 24 rows and you have completed the last row 4.

Start to decrease to turn heel: continue in the same decorative pattern to reinforce heel. Starting with a RS row, knit until there are 9 sts left on the LH needle. Decrease 1 st using skpo and turn work, leaving 7 sts on the other needle. S1 purlwise and purl until 9 sts remain on LH needle. P2tog and turn work. S1 and continue in decorative pattern until 8 sts remain on LH needle. Decrease using skpo and turn work. S1 purlwise and purl until 8 sts remain on LH needle. P2tog and turn work. Continue in the same way, reducing the number of sts at the sides on each row and keeping the same number of sts (8) in the middle.

When you run out of side sts, divide the heel flap sts between 2 needles (4–4). K4 to bring yarn to centre of heel, between needle 1 and needle 4.

FOOT

Pick up 14 sts from LH edge of heel flap using a spare needle. Knit the 4 sts from needle 1 and then the 14 picked up sts, turning sts knitwise. Work chart B1/B2 pattern on needles 2 and 3 starting with chart round 6. Pick up and knit 14 sts from RH edge of heel flap turning sts knitwise. Using the same needle, knit the 4 sts on needle 4 (59 sts).

Start gusset decrease: k2tog at end of needle 1, and ssk or skpo at beginning of needle 4 on every second round. Continue following chart pattern on needles 2 and 3 following chart B1/B2 and repeating rounds 1–20. Continue decreasing 2 gusset sts on every second round until there are 49 sts. For the right sock divide sts as follows: (13–11–12–13) and for the left sock as follows: (13–12–11–13).

Continue in st st on needles 1 and 4 and in chart pattern on needles 2 and 3. When you have knitted 45 rounds after the heel flap, and have completed chart round 10, change the number of sts on each needle as follows: (right: 12–12–13–12, left: 12–13–12–12) and start to decrease for the toe.

Work a wide wedge toe decrease on needles 1 and 4 and follow chart pattern on needles 2 and 3.

Needle 1: knit to last 3 sts, k2tog, k1.

Needle 4: k1, ssk, knit to end.

Work this decrease on every second round until there are 8 sts left on each needle. Then decrease on every round.

Needles 2 and 3: work toe decreases following chart C1/C2 (rounds 1–13).

Work until 9 sts remain. Break off yarn and thread through remaining sts.

Weave in ends and steam block lightly.

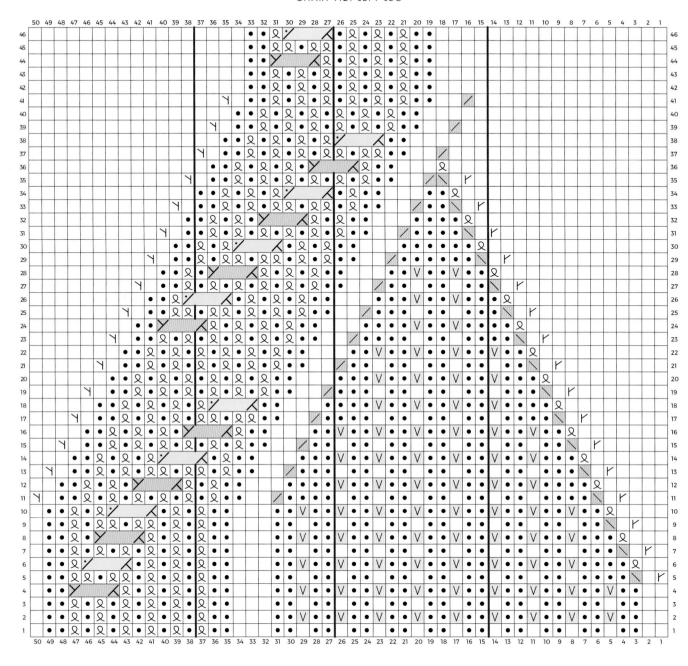

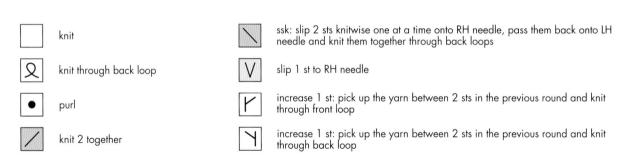

knit

knit through back loop

purl

knit 2 together

ssk: slip 2 sts knitwise one at a time onto RH needle, pass them back onto LH needle and knit them together through back loops

slip 1 st to RH needle

increase 1 st: pick up the yarn between 2 sts in the previous round and knit through front loop

increase 1 st: pick up the yarn between 2 sts in the previous round and knit through back loop

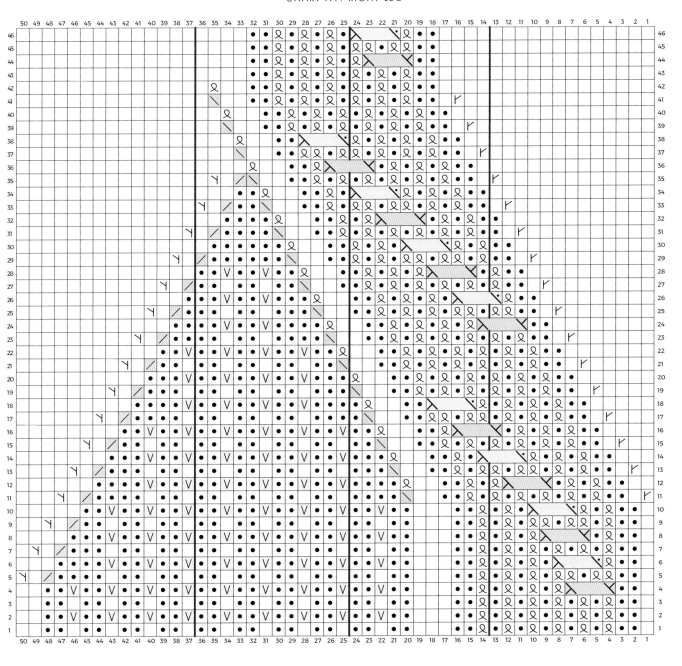

| | place 1 st on cable needle and bring to back of work, k1 through back loop, p1, k1 through back loop and k1 from cable needle | | next needle |
| place 1 st on cable needle and bring to back of work, k1 through back loop, p1, k1 through back loop and p1 from cable needle |
| place 3 sts on cable needle and bring to front of work, k1 and k1 from cable needle through back loop, p1, k1 through back loop |
| place 3 sts on cable needle and bring to front of work, p1 and k1 from cable needle through back loop, p1, k1 through back loop |
| slip 1 st knitwise, knit 2 together and pass the slipped st over the knitted sts |

CHART B2: LEFT FOOT

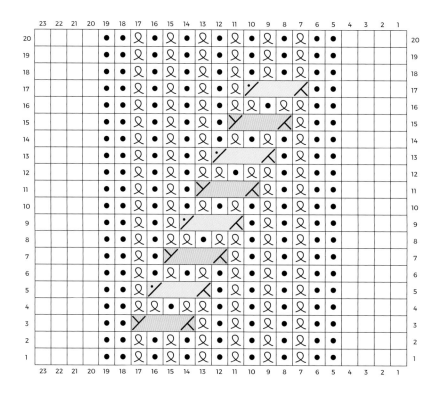

CHART B1: RIGHT FOOT

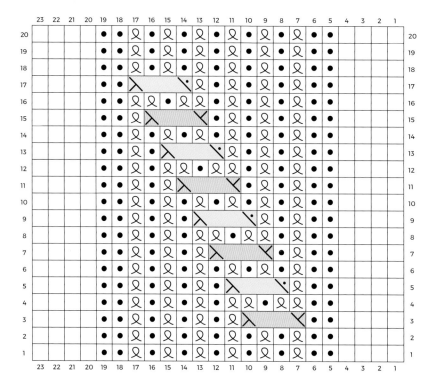

CHART C2:
LEFT TOE DECREASE

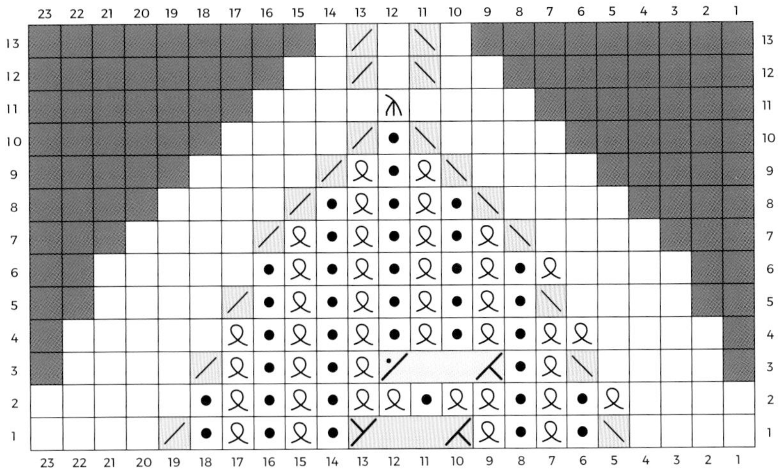

CHART C1:
RIGHT TOE DECREASE

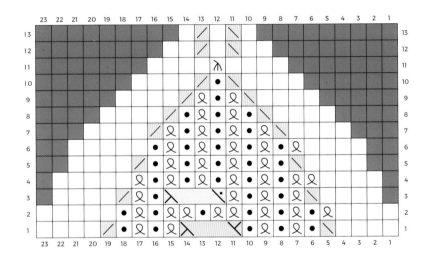

	knit
Q	knit through back loop
•	purl
/	knit 2 together
\	ssk: slip 2 sts knitwise one at a time onto RH needle, pass them back onto LH needle and knit them together through back loops
⋏	slip 1 st knitwise, knit 2 together and pass the slipped st over the knitted sts
	no st
	next needle

place 1 st on cable needle and bring to back of work, k1 through back loop, p1, k1 through back loop and k1 from cable needle

place 1 st on cable needle and bring to back of work, k1 through back loop, p1, k1 through back loop and p1 from cable needle

place 3 sts on cable needle and bring to front of work, k1 and k1 from cable needle through back loop, p1, k1 through back loop

place 3 sts on cable needle and bring to front of work, p1 and k1 from cable needle through back loop, p1, k1 through back loop

Christmas Eve

The best present at Christmas is unwrapping warm, woollen socks knitted especially for you. These socks are wonderful to relax in, enjoying a peaceful Christmas surrounded by the laughter of loved ones. Stop amid all the hustle and bustle and just be.

SIZE: UK 5/6 (Europe 38/39, US 7½/8½)

YARN: 2 balls of Gjestal Maija DK (8-ply/light worsted) yarn in Deep Red 237; 50g/130m/142yd

AMOUNT USED: 85g (3oz)

KNITTING NEEDLES: 3mm (UK 11, US 2/3) DPN or size to obtain correct tension

TENSION (GAUGE): 24 sts and 30 rows/ 10cm (4in)

LEG

Cast on 56 sts and divide between 4 needles as follows: 13–14–14–15. Join, being careful not to twist, and work in the round.

First work 2 rounds of rib as follows:
Needle 1: k2, p2, k2, p2, k2, p2, k1.
Needle 2: k3, p2, k9.
Needle 3: k9, p2, k3.
Needle 4: k1, p2, k2, p2, k2, p2, k2, p2.

After these 2 rounds, continue the rib pattern as set on needles 1 and 4 and start chart pattern on needles 2 and 3 following chart A. Start with chart round 1 and repeat chart rounds 1–14.

Continue until you have worked 43 rounds, including the rib, and completed chart round 13. Work one more round as follows: needle 1 in rib, needles 2 and 3 in pattern (chart round 14) and knit all sts on needle 4.

HEEL

Start decorative reinforced heel flap by knitting the sts on needle 1 onto needle 4 (28 sts for heel flap). Leave remaining sts on needles 2 and 3. Turn work, s1 purlwise and purl to end of row. Turn work.

Row 1 (RS): *s1, k1*, repeat from * to * to end of row. Turn work.
Row 2 (WS): s1 purlwise and purl to end of row. Turn work.
Row 3 (RS): s1, k1, *k1, s1*, repeat from * to * until 2 sts remain, k2 and turn work.
Row 4 (WS): s1 purlwise and purl to end of row. Turn work.
Repeat these four rows until the heel flap has 28 rows and you have completed the last row 4.

Start to decrease to turn heel: continue in the same decorative pattern to reinforce heel. Starting with a RS row, knit until there are 9 sts left on LH needle. Decrease 1 st using ssk or skpo and turn work, leaving 7 sts on the other needle. S1 purlwise and purl until 9 sts remain on LH needle. P2tog and turn work. S1 and continue in decorative pattern until there are 8 sts left on LH needle. Decrease using ssk or skpo and turn work. S1 purlwise and purl until 8 sts remain on LH needle. P2tog and turn work. Continue in the same way, reducing the number of sts at the sides on each row and keeping the same number of sts (12) in the middle.

When you run out of side sts, divide the heel flap sts between 2 needles (6–6). K6 to bring yarn to centre of heel, between needle 1 and needle 4.

FOOT

Pick up 16 sts from LH edge of heel flap using a spare needle. Knit the 6 sts from needle 1 and then the 16 picked up sts, turning sts knitwise. Work chart pattern on needles 2 and 3 starting with chart round 1. Pick up and knit 16 sts from RH edge of heel flap turning sts knitwise. Using the same needle, knit the 6 sts on needle 4 (72 sts).

Start gusset decrease: k2tog at end of needle 1, and ssk or skpo at beginning of needle 4 on every second round. Continue following chart pattern on needles 2 and 3. Continue decreasing 2 gusset sts on every second round until there are 56 sts (14–14–14–14). Continue in st st on needles 1 and 4 and in chart pattern on needles 2 and 3. When you have knitted 48 rounds after the heel flap, and have completed round 6 of the chart, start to decrease for the toe.

Work a wide wedge toe decrease on needles 1 and 4 and follow chart pattern on needles 2 and 3.
Needle 1: knit to last 3 sts, k2tog, k1.
Needle 4: k1, ssk, knit to end.
Work this decrease on every second round until there are 9 sts left on each needle. Then decrease on every round.
Needles 2 and 3: work toe decrease following chart B (chart rounds 1–16).
Work until 8 sts remain. Break off yarn and thread through remaining sts.

Weave in ends and steam block lightly.

CHART A

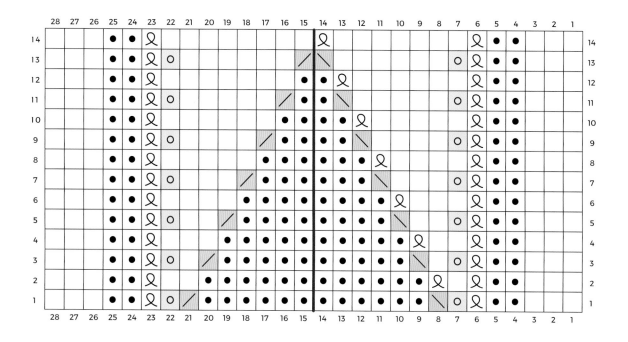

CHART B: TOE DECREASES

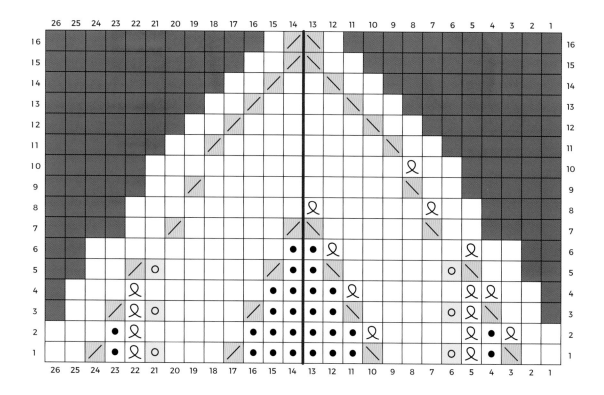

	knit		ssk: slip 2 sts knitwise one at a time onto RH needle, pass them back onto LH needle and knit them together through back loop
Ⴓ	knit through back loop		knit 2 together
●	purl		no st
○	yarn over		next needle

Secret Snowfall

Slowly, secretly, silently, true winter is here and the ground is wreathed in snowdrifts. Suddenly everything is soft and powdery; moments of happiness dusted with snowflakes and silent smiles in the evening dusk. The beautiful cable pattern on the leg gives this sock a touch of winter magic.

SIZE: UK 4 (Europe 37, US 6½) and UK 6 (Europe 39, US 8½)

YARN: 2 balls of Novita 7 Veljestä aran (10-ply/worsted) yarn in White 011; 100g/200m/218yd

AMOUNT USED: 120g (4¼oz)

KNITTING NEEDLES: 3.5mm (UK 9/10, US 4) DPN or size to obtain correct tension, cable needle

TENSION (GAUGE): 22 sts and 26 rows/10cm (4in)

BEFORE YOU START
Both sizes are knitted on the same number of sts until the gusset decrease. After that the differences for the larger size are shown in blue.

LEG

Cast on 52 sts and divide between 4 needles as follows: 11–16–14–11. Join, being careful not to twist, and work in the round.

Work all 50 rounds of chart B. Knit one more round, decreasing 4 sts (48 sts). Divide sts so there are 12 on each needle.

HEEL

Start the textured heel flap by knitting the sts on needle 1 onto needle 4 (24 sts for heel flap). Leave remaining sts on needles 2 and 3. Turn work and s1 purlwise, *p1, k1*, repeat from * to * until 4 sts remain, k1, p2tog, p1 (23 sts). Turn work.

Row 1 (RS): s1 knitwise, k1, *p1, s1 with yarn at front*, repeat from * to * until 3 sts remain, p1, k2 and turn work.
Row 2 (WS): s1 purlwise, *p1, k1*, repeat from * to * until 2 sts remain, p2.
Repeat these two rows until heel flap has 24 rows and you have completed the last WS row.

Start to decrease to turn heel on RS: s1 knitwise, *k1, p1* repeat from * to * until 8 sts remain, skpo and turn work. 6 sts remain on the other needle.
S1 purlwise and *k1, p1*, repeat from * to * until 8 sts remain on LH needle. P2tog and turn work.
S1 knitwise and *p1, k1*, repeat from * to * until 7 sts remain on LH needle, skpo and turn work.
S1 purlwise and *k1, p1*, repeat from * to * until 7 sts remain on LH needle. P2tog and turn work. Continue in the same way, reducing the number of sts at the sides on each row and keeping the same number of sts (9) in the middle.

When you run out of side sts, divide the heel flap sts between 2 needles (5–4). K3, k2tog on needle 4 to bring yarn to middle of heel.

FOOT

Pick up 14 sts from side of heel flap with needle 1 and pick up 14 sts from other side of heel flap with needle 4 (60 sts). Knit sts on needles 1 and 4 turning the picked up sts knitwise. Also knit sts on needles 2 and 3.

Start gusset decrease: k2tog at end of needle 1, and ssk or skpo at start of needle 4 on every second round. Once there are 44 sts left (10–12–12–10) – 48 sts (12–12–12–12), stop decreasing and continue in st st. For the smaller size, divide sts so there are 11 on each needle.

When you have worked 42 (46) rounds counted from edge of heel flap, start to decrease for the toe (wide wedge toe).
Needles 1 and 3: knit to last 3 sts, k2tog, k1.
Needles 2 and 4: k1, skpo, knit to end.
First work the decreases on every second round. Once there are 32 sts left (8–8–8–8), work the decreases on every round. When there are 8 sts left, break off yarn and thread through remaining sts.

Weave in ends and steam block lightly.

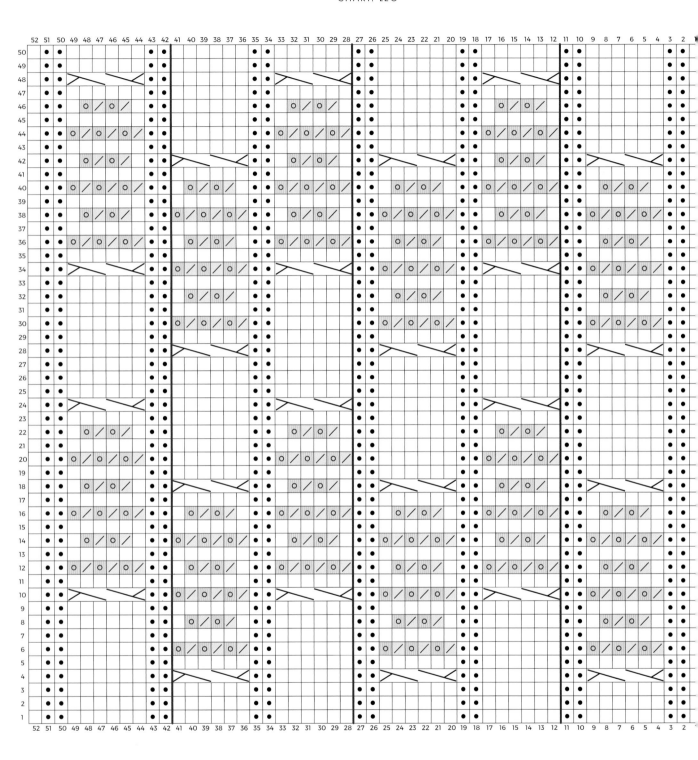

	knit
	purl
	knit 2 together
	yarn over
	place 3 sts on cable needle and bring to front of work, k3 and k3 from cable needle
	next needle

Snow Queen

*This design is for all the heroines in my life, my dear friends who make
every day a celebration. For people who are there when you need them,
whose words you can trust and who understand you even when you don't
understand yourself. These socks embody love and trust; pride in what you
have and who you are.*

SIZE: UK 6 (Europe 39, US 8½)

YARN: 2 balls of Gjestal Janne aran (10-ply/
worsted) yarn in Natural White 400 (A), 1 ball in
Basic Grey 405 (B) and 1 ball in Light Turquoise
490 (C); 50g/100m/109yd

AMOUNT USED: 130–140g (4½–5oz) A,
20–25g (¾–1oz) B, 20–25g (¾–1oz) C

KNITTING NEEDLES: 3.5mm (UK 9/10, US 4)
DPN or size to obtain correct tension, cable needle

TENSION (GAUGE): 20 sts and 26 rows/
10cm (4in)

BEFORE YOU START

The chart is read from bottom to top and from right
to left.

The instructions include two different sizes
(medium and wide). The width of the leg on chart A1
will fit a calf measuring about 35–39cm (13¾–15¼in)
and the width of the leg on chart A2 will fit a calf
measuring about 40–45cm (15¾–17¾in). The heel
and foot are knitted following the same instructions
for both sizes.

LEG (MEDIUM)

Cast on 64 sts in yarn A and divide sts between 4 needles as follows: 15–17–16–16. Join, being careful not to twist, and work in the round. Work rib following rounds 1–10 of chart A1. Work round 11 in st st, increasing 1 st at the same time, and check that sts are divided between needles as follows: 16–17–16–16.

Start the Fair Isle pattern at round 12 of chart A1 and work leg following chart, decreasing in a suitable place at beginning of needle 1 and end of needle 4 on the following rounds:

Decreases:
Round 48: decrease 2 sts (63 sts).
Round 60: decrease 2 sts (61 sts).
Note: on round 66, divide sts between needles as follows: 18–13–12–18.
Round 67: decrease 2 sts (59 sts).
Round 73: decrease 2 sts (57 sts).
Round 78: decrease 2 sts (55 sts).
Round 83: decrease 2 sts (53 sts).
Round 88: decrease 2 sts (51 sts).

When you have worked all 102 rounds for the leg, check that sts are divided between needles as follows: 13–13–12–13.

LEG (WIDE)

Cast on 70 sts in yarn A and divide sts between 4 needles as follows: 18–18–17–17. Join, being careful not to twist, and work in the round. Work rib following rounds 1–10 of chart A2. Work round 11 in st st. At the same time, increase 3 sts and check that sts are divided between needles as follows: 18–19–18–18.

Start the Fair Isle pattern at round 12 of chart A2 and work leg following chart, decreasing in a suitable place at beginning of needle 1 and end of needle 4 on the following rounds:

Decreases:
Round 34: decrease 2 sts (71 sts).
Round 48: decrease 2 sts (69 sts).
Round 54: decrease 2 sts (67 sts).
Round 60: decrease 2 sts (65 sts).

Note: on round 66, divide sts between needles as follows: 20–13–12–20.
Round 67: decrease 2 sts (63 sts).
Round 72: decrease 2 sts (61 sts).
Round 76: decrease 2 sts (59 sts).
Round 80: decrease 2 sts (57 sts).
Round 84: decrease 2 sts (55 sts).
Round 88: decrease 2 sts (53 sts).
Round 91: decrease 2 sts (51 sts).

When you have worked all 102 rounds for the leg, check that sts are divided between needles as follows: 13–13–12–13.

HEEL

Start ribbed heel flap in yarn A by knitting the sts on needle 1 onto needle 4 (26 sts). Leave remaining sts on needles 2 and 3. Turn work, s1 purlwise and purl to end of row. At the same time, increase 2 sts making 24 sts for heel flap. Turn work.

Row 1 (RS): *s1, k1*, repeat from * to * to end of row. Turn work.
Row 2 (WS): s1 purlwise, p1, *k1, p1*, repeat from * to * to end of row.
Repeat these two rows until heel flap has 24 rows and you have completed the last WS row.

Start to decrease to turn heel: continue in the same rib pattern to reinforce heel. Starting with a RS row, knit until there are 9 sts left on the LH needle, skpo and turn work, leaving 7 sts on the other needle. S1 purlwise, and continue in reinforced heel pattern until 9 sts remain on LH needle. P2tog and turn work. S1 knitwise and continue in rib pattern until 8 sts remain on LH needle, skpo and turn work. S1 purlwise, and continue in rib pattern until 8 sts remain on LH needle. P2tog and turn work. Continue in the same way, reducing the number of sts at the sides on each row and keeping the same number of sts (8) in the middle.

When you run out of side sts, divide the heel flap sts between 2 needles (4–4). Knit 4 sts on needle 4 to bring yarn between needles 4 and 1.

FOOT

Pick up 14 sts from side of heel flap with needle 1 and pick up 14 sts from other side of heel flap with needle 4 (61 sts). Continue Fair Isle pattern following chart B from round 1. Knit the sts picked up from the edge of the heel flap, turning sts knitwise.

Start gusset decrease: k2tog at end of needle 1 and ssk or skpo at beginning of needle 4 on rounds as shown in chart B (rounds 2, 4, 6, 8, 10 and 12). The dark grey squares on the chart represent places where there are no sts. After the gusset decrease there will be 49 sts (12–13–12–12).

Continue the Fair Isle pattern following the chart. On round 28, decrease 1 st at end of needle 4 and divide sts so there are 12 sts on each needle.

When you have worked all 38 rounds of chart B, start to decrease for the toe. The Fair Isle pattern continues for another 6 rounds while working the toe decrease (chart rounds 39–44). When you reach the end of the chart, there will be 36 sts (9–9–9–9).

Finish sock with a wide wedge toe in yarn A, decreasing every round:
Needles 1 and 3: knit to last 3 sts, k2tog, k1.
Needles 2 and 4: k1, ssk or skpo, knit to end.
When there are 8 sts left, break off yarn and thread through remaining sts.

Weave in ends and steam block lightly.

CHART A1: MEDIUM LEG

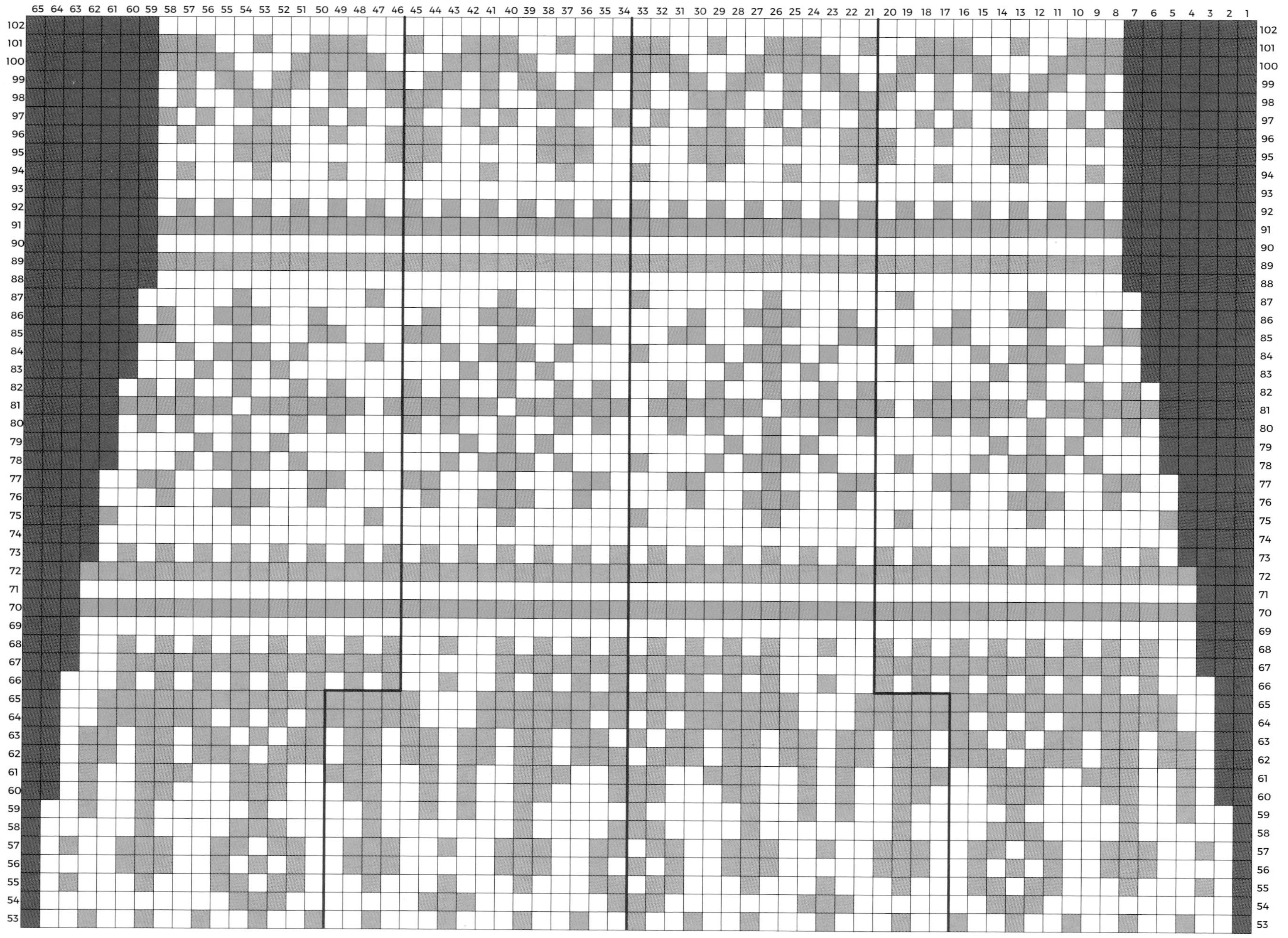

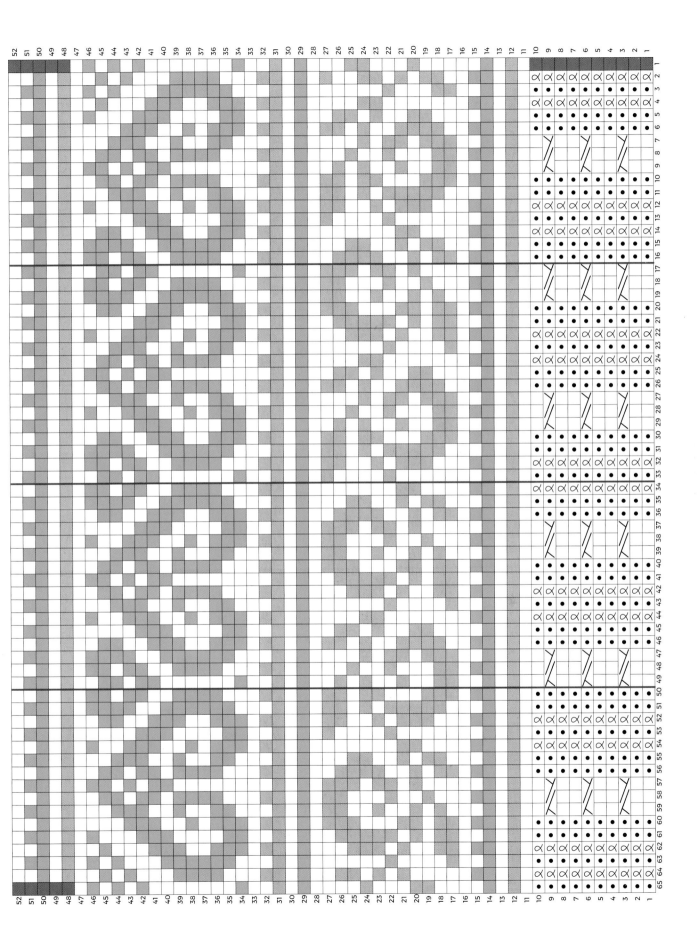

CHART A2: WIDE LEG

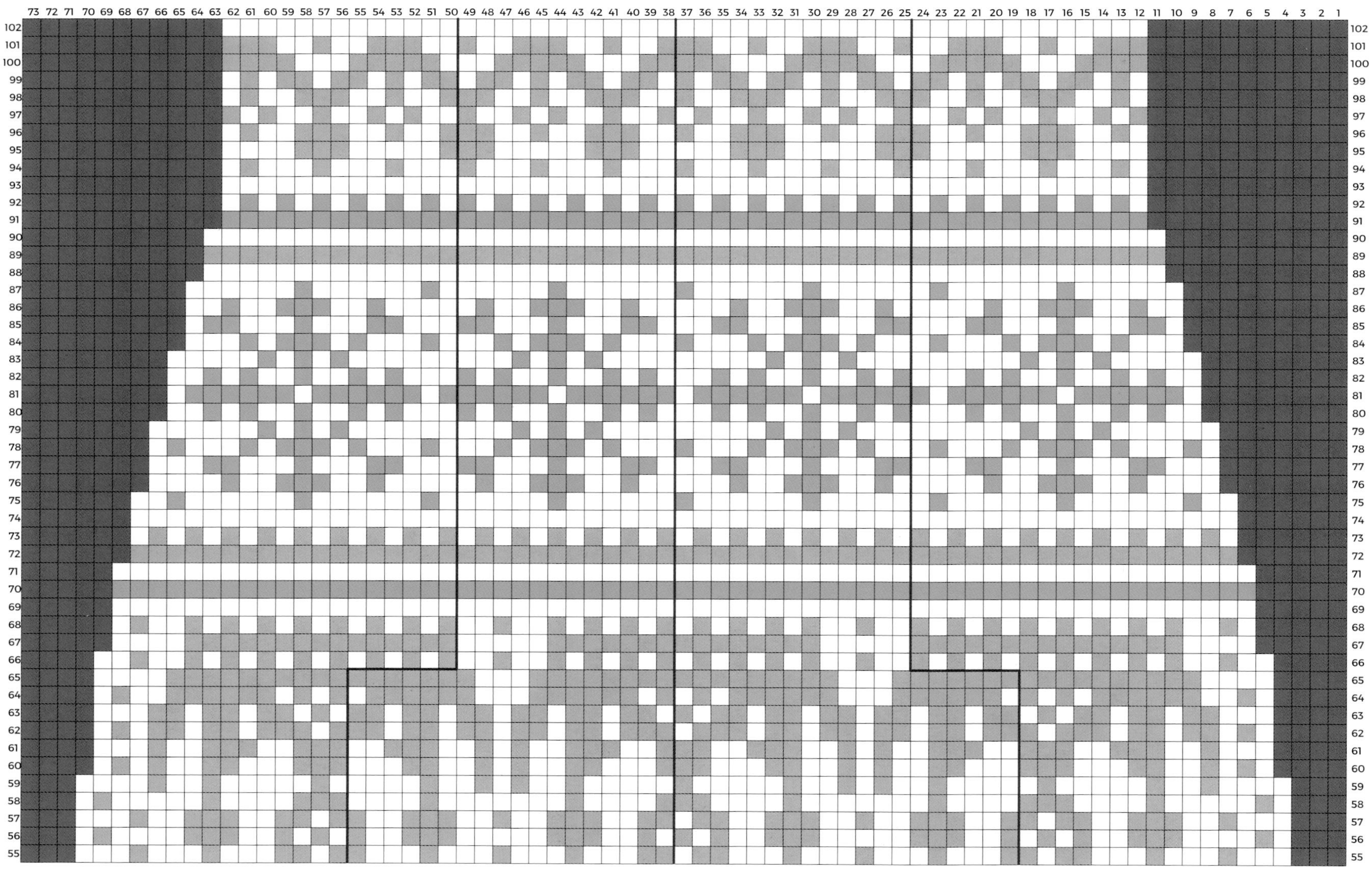

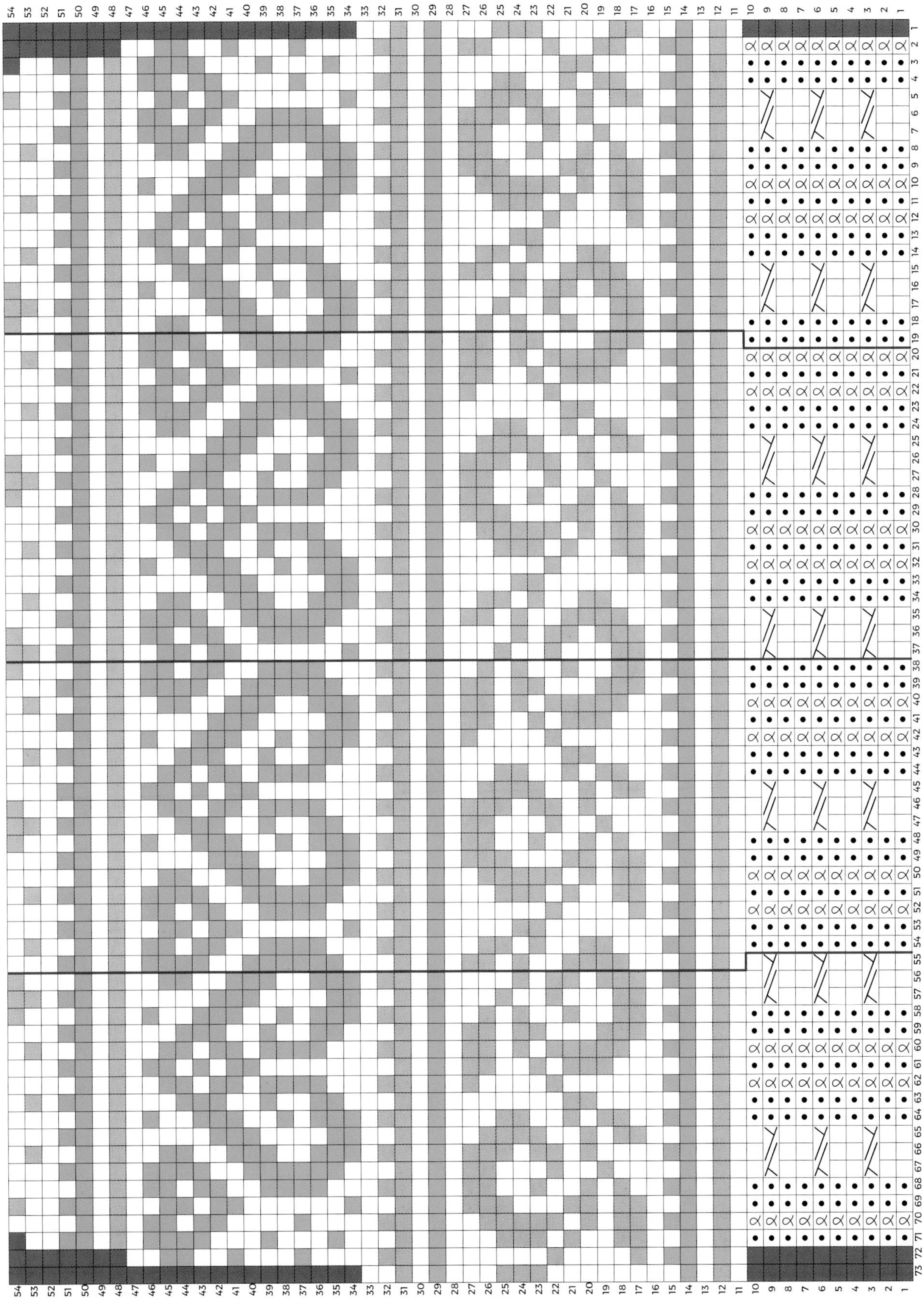

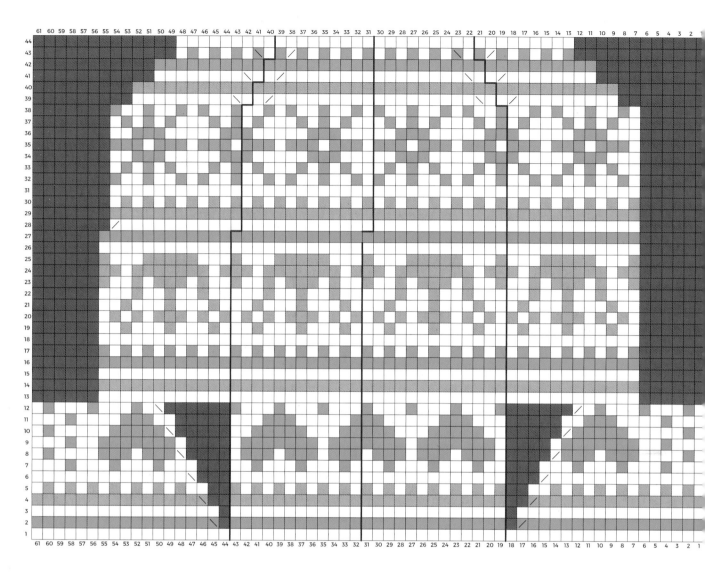

	knit (in yarn A)		place 1 st on cable needle and bring to front of work, k2 and k1 from cable needle (in yarn A)
	knit (in yarn B)		knit 2 together (in yarn B)
	knit (in yarn C)		ssk: slip 2 sts knitwise one at a time onto RH needle, pass them back onto LH needle and knit them together through back loops (in yarn B)
ℚ	knit through back loop (in yarn A)		knit 2 together (in yarn C)
•	purl (in yarn A)		ssk: slip 2 sts knitwise one at a time onto RH needle, pass them back onto LH needle and knit them together through back loops (in yarn C)
	no st		knit 2 together (in yarn A)
	next needle		ssk: slip 2 sts knitwise one at a time onto RH needle, pass them back onto LH needle and knit them together through back loops (in yarn A)